F   cop. 1
HOW

HOWE
God, the universe and hot
fudge

F   cop. 1
HOW
HOWE
God, the universe and hot fudge
sundaes   11.95

DATE DUE	BORROWER'S NAME	ROOM NUMBER
OCT 2 8 '85	Erica Dupar	T-3
		8
NOV 1 2 '85	Ruth Pacheco	
NOV 2 6 '85		8
DEC 1 7 '85	Ruth Pacheco	

GOD,
the UNIVERSE,
and Hot Fudge Sundaes

GOD, the UNIVERSE, and Hot Fudge Sundaes

A novel by Norma Howe

Houghton Mifflin Company
Boston
1984

Grateful acknowledgement is given for permission to quote from *Cosmos,* copyright
© 1980 by Carl Sagan Productions, Incorporated. By permission of the author and his
agents, Scott Meredith Literary Agency, Incorporated, 845 Third Avenue, New York,
New York 10022.

Library of Congress Cataloging in Publication Data

Howe, Norma.
  God, the universe, and hot fudge sundaes.

  Summary: Troubled by her younger sister's death and her parents' separation, six-
teen-year-old Alfie makes friends with a college student named Kurt who helps her
decide what she really believes about life, death, religion, and reason.
   I. Title.
PZ7.H8376Go 1984   [Fic]   83-26548
ISBN 0-395-35483-8

F How c.1

Printed in the United States of America

S 10 9 8 7 6 5 4 3 2 1

For old Green-eyes

God,
the UNIVERSE,
and Hot Fudge Sundaes

1

EXCEPT FOR LORI GAYE AND GEORGINA Hinde, I'm the only girl in the Math Club. And Lori doesn't count, of course, and neither does Georgina, really. Lori would join the Gutter Gum-Scrapers Club if there were guys in it, and Georgina's only there because Jason is. Georgina and Jason have been stuck to each other like glue since last October. They're always holding hands, or their thumbs are stuck in each other's back pockets, or they're joined at the ankles or something. That's how they sit at Math Club meetings — with their ankles crossed.

But I guess everyone has some kind of aberration. Take me, for instance. I can't swear. No kidding. No matter how hard I try, I just can't do it. I can't even say *hell* or *damn*, for gods' sake. And make it sound right, I mean. I'm really warped that way. I still embarrass myself thinking about the last time I tried. It was in gym class and there was something wrong with the heater. It was about one hundred fifty degrees in there. We were supposed to be playing badminton, but we were actually just standing around in a circle, half-heartedly swatting the birdie at each other.

I decided it was then or never. I was determined to go through with it. I gritted my teeth and counted to myself, "One, two, three!" Then I blurted out, "Gees, it's hot as hell in here!"

Well, I knew it was a mistake as soon as I said it. You should have seen the looks I got. First of all, Bonnie and Marcie — they're two girls from church that I used to go around with before I met Tyler — well, they just whispered something to each other and turned away. Then Debbie Covell — she's head cheerleader this year — she put her hand over her mouth, snickered, and said, "Ohh, Alfie! What you said!" And the others all laughed at me.

All that just goes to prove how hard it is to get out of your pigeonhole. Once a Bible-bunny, always a Bible-bunny. *Bible-bunny* is Tyler's phrase. My dad heard her say it once and thought it was really funny. Now he goes around saying it all the time.

My dad's got an aberration. He's a punster. That's his main one anyway. He makes these really terrible puns and thinks he's so clever. When I told him the Math Club tied for first place at the last Mathlete, he got this *look* on his face and said slyly, "Well, that figures." Sometimes I think that self-satisfied look is even harder to take than the puns.

My dad's a bureaucrat for the state of California. He works in the Justice Department. I think his job is probably pretty boring. That's why he makes puns and goes jogging a lot. And my mom drives him crazy, that's for sure.

My mom now, well, her aberration is a little more complicated than not being able to swear or making puns all the time. Actually, a lot of people wouldn't call it an aberration at all. The thing is, she talks to Jesus Christ and is waiting for Him to return out of the clouds, just like it says in the Bible. The reason I call that an aberration is because I don't think He's coming back. Not anymore, I don't. I just recently made up my mind about that, and this time I think it's for good.

My friend Tyler doesn't have any aberration at all, and that's the truth. She's really neat, that's all I can say. She's the friend I always dreamed of having, but never thought I'd find. I only wish everyone could have a best friend like her at least once in life. Tyler doesn't swear as much as most of the kids at school, but at least she can do it when she wants to — and make it sound right, too.

My other favorite person, besides Tyler, is Mr. Burr. He's our Math Club advisor and I have him for calculus this year. Actually, he's my all-time favorite teacher. I talk to Mr. Burr a lot about my problems. "Uncle Freddy" we call him. But not to his face. At least, not until we graduate. After they graduate, all the kids come back and say, "Hi, Uncle Freddy. How's it going?" Oh, a few kids still going here call him Uncle Freddy to his face, but I suppose you're always going to find kids like that around — kids who just don't understand life's little subtleties.

I usually see Mr. Burr two or three times a day. I have him first period for calculus (I'm only a junior, but I'm way ahead in math), and then I'm his assistant during his preparation period. I get three credits for that, but I earn them. I tutor kids sometimes, and I help grade homework papers and all kinds of stuff. You don't just sign up to be his assistant, either. You're chosen. It's really quite an honor. This year the choice was between me and this very smart friend of Tyler's, Victor Beauchamp. I don't know what it is with Victor, but he has this way of looking right through you, like you're not there.

Mr. Burr had called both of us in when school started last September and said, "Well kids, I'll take one of you first semester and the other one second semester. Shall we toss a coin? Leave it to chance?''

We looked around at each other; then out of the blue Victor said in an amateurish Italian accent, ''Chance is just a foolish name for fate.'' I burst out laughing. Mr. Burr looked puzzled, but I knew right away it was a sort of punchline spoken by an Italian gigolo in an old Fred Astaire movie I had seen once on the ''Late, Late Show.''

I had a sneaking suspicion that Victor thought I was laughing for nothing, without really getting the joke, so I repeated something I had heard from my father. ''You know,'' I said, ''that reminds me of this guy who had to spend the entire night at the top of the Empire State Building. The elevator was broken and he was a-fred a-staires.''

Victor didn't exactly laugh at that, but his expression changed, and for the first time he really looked at me. Victor's eyes are a brooding greenish-blue, like the inner curve of a breaking wave on a late afternoon at the beach, when the sun has disappeared behind a cloud and the wind has suddenly come up. Actually, I've given quite a lot of thought to Victor's eyes.

''He was a-fred a-staires, huh?'' Victor said, deadpan. ''Yeah, I heard about that guy.''

Mr. Burr was looking alternately at me and at Victor, watching us in an amused kind of way. ''You know,'' he said, ''I have a strange feeling I'm in the wrong room, somehow.'' He reached in his pocket and got out a coin. ''Call it,'' he said. ''The winner's my first semester assistant.'' Victor won the toss, but now we're in the second semester, and it's my turn.

I was really looking forward to seeing Mr. Burr again, because I had just missed over a week of school and a lot of things had happened to me. We didn't get to talk much dur-

4

ing calculus, but I found him seventh period — his free period — in the computer room, as usual. He was drinking coffee out of his Thermos and reading the *Chronicle*.

"Hi, Mr. Burr," I said.

"Oh. It's you." He always acts like I'm a big pest.

I was relieved that he seemed about the same as always, though. I had been a little afraid that he might act different because of everything that had happened.

He glanced up at me and then started reading the paper again.

"How's it going, Alfie?" he asked, turning a page. He always says, "How's it going?"

"Fine."

"Oh, yeah?"

"Well, it's better, at least."

He gave me a funny look and put down the *Chron*. He unscrewed the lid of his Thermos and shook out the last few drops. He closed one eye and looked down into the Thermos bottle, as if he didn't believe it was empty. Then he kind of smiled at me and put the lid back on. He leaned back in his chair and ran his hand through his hair, watching me. He's got blond kinky hair that juts out all over the place. It always makes me think that it's his brains there, overflowing out of his skull, all wild and unruly. He still didn't say anything. He just looked at me and raised his eyebrows.

I had to smile. "There's this lady in my mom's Bible Study Group," I explained. "Whenever you ask her how she is, she says, 'Oh, I'm better.' So, of course, you have to say, 'Oh, have you been sick?' And then she gets to tell you all about her arthritis and stuff."

"Ah, I see." Mr. Burr paused. "So how's your arthritis?"

"My arthritis is fine. You want to hear something funny though?"

He looked sort of surprised. "Funny? Sure. Let's hear something funny."

"Well, you know, until pretty recently, I thought my big problem was that I was crazy."

"Yeah. I know all about that," he said, yawning, pretending he was bored.

"Well, lately, since Francie's funeral and everything — well, I've changed my mind. I don't know when it happened, exactly, maybe it was actually pretty gradual, you know?"

Mr. Burr looked up quickly when I mentioned my little sister Francie's funeral. I think he was probably checking to see if I was all right. To see if I was going to break down or something. Which I wasn't. I definitely wasn't going to do that. So he just said, "Don't say *you know* all the time. Go on."

"So anyway," I continued, "you know — whoops! Anyway, now I think that I'm probably okay. It's everybody else that's nuts."

Mr. Burr sighed. "I know the feeling."

"But before," I continued, taking a big breath, "when I thought it was just me, it was easier, see? I thought, well gee, all I have to do is quit being so crazy and I'll be okay. But now. . . ." I faltered.

"You can't change the whole world, right? You're trapped in a world of ding-a-lings."

I nodded. "Yep. I guess that's right."

Neither of us said anything after that. I started punching stuff into the computer, just fooling around.

Pretty soon I said, "Hey, Mr. Burr, can I ask you something?"

He gave me an exasperated look. That meant yes, so I asked him.

"Do you believe in the devil?"

He looked really surprised. "The devil?"

6

"Yeah. And angels. Like Billy Graham. Do you believe in angels and the devil?"

He didn't answer right away. He sort of thought about it for a minute. Then he asked, "Do you mean philosophically, the concept of devils and angels, or do you mean that sinister guy in red underwear and those fat little baby-things with wings?"

I laughed. "Come on, Mr. Burr."

He cleared his throat. "Well, do you believe in them, Alfie?"

"Not lately," I said. I quit playing around with the computer and leaned my chin in my hand. "Mr. Burr, do you realize that we're surrounded by people who believe in devils and angels? Do you realize we're surrounded by people who believe in horoscopes and in their biorhythms, for gods' sake? Sometimes I think I'm going nuts."

"I thought you just said everybody else was nuts."

I smiled. "Did I?"

We didn't talk for a few minutes. Mr. Burr was just gazing out the window and I was sitting there, waiting to see if he was going to say anything more on the subject. Pretty soon he did.

"You know, Alfie," he began, "I think you're making short shrift of religion when you just lump it indiscriminately with things like astrology and —" he waved his hand in the air — "and biorhythms and such."

"Really?"

"Yes. I think so. In my church, for example, we deal more in terms of the *idea* of good and evil. That is, we don't interpret the Bible —"

"You go to church?" I asked, interrupting.

He gave me a stern look. "Don't interrupt me when I'm speaking."

"Oh. Sorry."

"As I was saying," he enunciated slowly, "we don't interpret the Bible literally in every instance."

"Oh."

"Now, what were you asking?"

"Well," I said, "I was just asking if you went to church, that's all."

"Yes, I go to church."

"How often?"

"Often enough," he said. Then he laughed. "Hey, 'I didn't expect the Spanish Inquisition!'" he said, imitating that Monty Python program where the Inquisitors keep popping up in every sketch.

I smiled. "That's pretty good, Mr. Burr." Then I got serious. "But really, do you *really* read the Bible? Have you ever read The Revelation?"

"Well sure. I have read the Bible, certainly. Not as much as I should, probably." He hesitated. "But I do read it, on occasion."

"Do you believe all those prophesies in The Revelation?" I asked. "Do you believe that everyone's name is written in the Lamb's Book of Life, until some are blotted out, and that the Antichrist is going to rule —"

"Hold it, Alfie."

Now *he* was interrupting.

"I think we may be getting on touchy ground here." He pursed his lips and then rubbed them together. "I mean, I don't think it's a very good idea for me to delve too deeply into religion — or politics, for that matter — with my students. I just don't think it's a good policy. So I'll tell you what. You come back in a year or two, after you graduate, when you're a real person," he winked, "and we'll knock it around then? How's that?"

8

I sighed. "Okay. Just when it's beginning to get interesting."

I started punching stuff into the computer again, and Mr. Burr was balancing his chair on its back legs now, just kind of playing around. Suddenly he leaned forward quickly and the front legs of his chair hit the floor with a jolt.

"How are your parents, Alfie?"

"What?"

"Your mother and father. How are they doing?"

"They're okay, I guess. You mean because of Francie? Well, it's not that we didn't have any warning, or anything. . . ."

He nodded. "I guess that's true."

"But boy," I said, "I sure don't know what's going to happen now."

Mr. Burr looked up. "Oh?"

I was kind of sorry I had blurted that out. I didn't really intend to get into all that, I mean about my parents and all that. Gees, I hadn't even talked to anyone about it yet, not even Tyler. But the truth was, it was pretty obvious to me that my parents — well, since Francie died and Aunt Marion moved away, my parents have hardly even spoken to each other. Oh, they're polite and everything, I don't mean that. It's just that they don't really talk. It's like they're on TV or something, with their lines all written out. They're just going through the motions.

I don't know how, but Mr. Burr seemed to sense all that. Maybe something happened at the funeral. He went to the funeral. That was probably it. Maybe he noticed how they don't even touch each other, for gods' sake. You wouldn't have to be a genius to notice that.

Suddenly my chest was starting to fill up with that scared and lonely and helpless feeling again. I felt myself starting to cry. God, I didn't want to start anything like that in front of Mr. Burr, but I couldn't help it. I began biting the inside of my cheek real hard. I hoped that the pain could help me forget about crying, but it didn't work. I guess I really lost control then. I put my head in my hands and started brushing the tears away. Then I muttered something like, "God, my whole *fam*ily's falling apart!"

Mr. Burr didn't try to stop me from crying. He didn't say "Don't cry now," or "Stop crying," or any of that useless stuff. He did go looking through his desk drawers for some Kleenex though. He found a box and put it on top of the desk. "Here," he said, nudging me. "Wipe your eyes."

Then he started talking. "Okay Alfie," he said, "listen to me a minute. You've been through a lot lately, right?"

I nodded.

"And now you're worried about your parents, right?"

I nodded again.

"Okay. You're sixteen. Seventeen?"

"Almost."

"Okay. Almost seventeen. So listen, no matter what your parents do, they're adults. They have their own lives to lead. Just like you have yours. What they do is going to affect you, naturally. Because you love them, right?"

"Uh-huh."

"But here's the thing, Alfie. You're your own person now. You're really not a little girl anymore. Heck, you'll be going away to college in a little more than a year. . . ." He seemed to be running out of steam. "You see what I'm getting at?"

The funny thing is, I think I did. "Like, this is their problem. Is that what you mean?"

Mr. Burr took a deep breath. He seemed really quite relieved. "You got it. It's their problem. You've put your finger on it exactly."

I blew my nose a couple of times. "Boy, I said, "life is so crazy!"

Mr. Burr looked at me real sympathetically. It made me feel good, you know? I could tell he was concerned about me. It makes you feel good when you know someone you like really cares about you. Then he said, "Sure. Lots of it is crazy. Lots of it isn't. Like math, for instance. Math's not crazy, is it?"

"Well, sure," I admitted, "but math's not life. Math is just . . . math. But life is crazy. People are crazy. God, everything's just so mixed up. . . ."

Mr. Burr stood up and put his hands in his pockets and started walking around the room. "Well, you're right, of course. Sometimes things can seem pretty mixed up. But then, they usually have a way of straightening out again. This just happens to be a very rough time for you. But listen, Alfie, you're a very bright and level-headed young lady. I feel quite confident that you'll come through this okay."

I looked up when he called me bright and level-headed. Mr. Burr generally didn't give outright compliments like that. I didn't know what to say.

He smiled at me. "Come on. Get your things together. I've got to stop by the post office. I'll give, you a ride home."

No one was home when I got there, and that was a very strange feeling. Francie's wheelchair was in its usual place by the hallway closet. Aunt Marion no longer lives with us. She moved out right after the funeral two days ago. Dad was probably still at work. He's kind of a workaholic. And, since it was Wednesday, Mom was no doubt at Wednesday Bible Study.

Thinking about Wednesday Bible Study just reminded me

of this crazy understanding I used to have with Jesus, before I called it off. It was this: I don't think I really expected that He would actually come back like the Bible said He would, but in case He did, in case He did return, floating out of the clouds like a thief in the night when I least expected Him, He would forgive me for not really expecting Him! He would place His billowy-clad arm gently around my shoulder and whisper to me, "I don't blame you, my child." He would give a kind of holy chuckle and say, "I wouldn't have believed it either."

That's what He would have said to me, more or less. As you can see, I must have been really nuts.

2

SOMETIMES, WHEN I HAVE LOTS OF TROU-
bles, I like to lie in bed dreaming up miraculous acne cures. I like to think about my
Miracle Vacuum Cure the most. All you do is vacuum your
face with this special vacuum I invented. It looks something
like my dad's safety razor, but it's really a magical vacuum
that simply whisks away all your blemishes. After the initial
treatment, you need maintenance vacuuming every two weeks.

My Miracle Lotion Cure takes longer. First, you have to
spread the lotion. I invented that, too. Its secret ingredients
have astounded the medical world. It's made up of Nacho
Cheese Puffs and Hershey's chocolate syrup, mixed in the
blender. After you spread it on, it takes quite a while to dry,
and it's quite painful. You know it's done its work when it
turns from brown to a kind of murky green. That's all the
impurities, you see, all dissolved and brought to the surface
and ready to be whisked away with a rinse of warm Dr. Pep-
per. You look in the mirror and are amazed and astounded by
your new cover-girl complexion. The Miracle Lotion Cure
needs to be repeated once a month.

My Miracle Pill Cure is the most controversial. First, you must secure an okay from Washington. The government is quite sure that the Miracle Pill is absolutely safe, but there are a lot of problems with the dermatologists. Most dermatologists argue that this pill is Extremely Dangerous, but the consumer groups say the dermatologists are just afraid of losing all their teen-aged customers. Sometimes I am the president of the most influential consumer group, and I go around the country debating the infamous Dr. Zits, who represents the dermatologists. I do an outstanding job, and Washington finally okays the pill. They send the first one to me. I swallow it over national TV, probably on "Good Morning, America." One Miracle Pill is all it takes. You swallow it and you're cured of acne forever. Instantly, and forever. Hey — that's a great name for the pill! The Instantly and Forever Miracle Acne Pill.

My dad never did come home that night. That's not unusual though. He has quite a few meetings in San Francisco and places, and lots of times he stays over for a couple of days. So Mom and I were home alone together.

After Mr. Burr dropped me off and while I was waiting for her to get home from Wednesday Bible Study, I started reading some stuff in *Cosmos,* the book by Carl Sagan that my dad had given me the week before. I was rereading the stuff about black holes and thinking about Francie and an idea I had the first time I read about them. It was actually pretty crazy what I was thinking — that when you die, maybe what happens is some invisible part of you hurtles through space, attracted by some yet undiscovered force, and you are sucked through a black hole and come out on the other side of time and space, so to speak, in a brand new dimension and have a grand reunion with those who have gone before.

What it boils down to is that I was daydreaming that, somehow, I might — just might — get to see Francie again.

My mom finally came home with Mrs. Snyder about five o'clock. Mrs. Millie Snyder is one of my mom's spirit-filled sisters. That's what my mom calls them. It means that they've all been born again. There's Mrs. Snyder, Ginnie Rogers, old Mrs. Thompson (the one with the arthritis), a ding-bat lady named Belle Jorgenson, Mrs. Arnold, and three or four others. The only man in the group is Pastor Huggins. As my dad has said on several occasions, Mom thinks Pastor Huggins is the cat's meow.

Well, Mrs. Snyder has this son named Gregg. Gregg, unfortunately, is in love with me. Gregg's okay, I don't mean he isn't, it's just that he's not my type, that's all. He and his mom were about the first people we met when we moved here from Van Nuys four years ago. Gregg's father is divorced from his mother. He's an airline pilot for TWA and came under the influence of the devil — in the form of a young stewardess from Iowa or somewhere. That's what Mrs. Snyder told me once after a Wednesday Bible Study at our house. Everyone else had gone home and Mrs. Snyder was helping me and Mom clean up the dishes. It was kind of cozy, and I guess she figured I was grown up enough to discuss such topics. She told me her husband was not strong enough to overcome the devil's urgings. She's really pretty bitter about the whole thing.

The Snyders live down in the next block. Gregg doesn't go to my school, thank God. I mean if he did, he'd just be hanging around me all the time. He goes to a dumpy little religious school not too far from here. For a while I thought my mom was going to make me go there, too. At least she was talking about it. This was when I started high school. Boy, I was really scared. They don't even have computers over there, for gods' sake.

I guess I should interrupt myself to tell you right now that I don't consider saying "for gods' sake" swearing. But my mom does. I wrote it down and showed her the small *g* and how it was plural and all. I told her I meant the old Roman gods, and stuff like that. But she still doesn't like it. Mom gives me a bad time about saying "gees" all the time too. She thought "gees" was short for Jesus. But I convinced her that when I say it, it only means *g*, but plural. Like one gee, two gees.

Anyway, about the Christian school, my dad came to my rescue, as usual. Whenever I have any trouble like that with Mom, my dad usually comes to my rescue. He said I didn't have to go there if I didn't want to. My dad always has the last word. First comes God, then Dad, then Mom, then me. That's what it says in the Bible. So my mom smiles gamely and goes along with it. Sometimes she really hates it though, when Dad wants something different from what she wants. That's when she refers to him as "my *hus*band" in a real bitter, mocking tone of voice. About the Christian school, I overheard her tell Mrs. Snyder, "Well, I'd like to send Alfie there, but my *hus*band says she can go where she chooses."

Anyway, I put *Cosmos* away when I saw Mrs. Snyder's car pull in the driveway and I went into the kitchen and got a Coke.

They came in the front door and Mrs. Snyder went right to the den to phone Gregg and tell him where she was. Mom came into the kitchen. I could tell right away that she was worried about something. I could tell by her eyes. Whenever Mom is extra worried or has some big problem, her eyes get a kind of ethereal look about them. It's hard to explain. They fog over. And she smiles a kind of weird, incongruous smile. When my dad is the cause of the problem, which is quite often the case, he calls it her martyred look. "There she goes," he says to the wall. "There she goes with that martyred look." And then my mom adds to that another kind of smile, an innocent, puzzled look of wonderment, as if she's saying, "What on earth are you talking about?"

She walked over and kissed me on the cheek. She was wearing her navy blue skirt with a red and white polka dot blouse. She looked nice. She always does. "Hi, dear," she said. "Have a good day?"

"Uh-huh. Pretty good."

She rinsed her hands in the sink and got her white apron out and tied it on. "I thought we could have a tuna salad for dinner. Does that sound all right?"

"Oh, sure."

She called out to Mrs. Snyder, who was still talking softly on the phone. "Millie? Would you like to stay for dinner? Alfie and I are just going to have a little salad — nothing elaborate." Then she added, "Maybe Gregg would like to come over, too."

"Well," came the voice from the den, uncertain. "Well, I'll ask." A few seconds later she called out, "Yes, Virginia, he says he'd love to come. He'll be right over."

Then she hung up the phone and came into the kitchen. She looked at me a little haughtily, but that didn't surprise me. She doesn't really like me too much. I think she's afraid I'm going to steal Gregg away from her.

"Well, he*llo* there, Alfreda!" She always calls me Alfreda. I hate it.

Mrs. Snyder cleared her throat. She has this kind of gratey little voice. "My Gregg tells me that was quite a trip you young people took last weekend. And who is this boy *Kurt* that Gregg is telling me about?"

She would have to bring up Kurt. "Oh, he's just a student over at Davis, a graduate student. . . ."

"Oh, he's older then?" Boy, I didn't like her tone one bit. Mom noticed it, too. She glanced at me, questioning, concerned. I met her gaze squarely. "It's okay, Mom," I said softly.

"How old *is* he?" Mrs. Snyder just wouldn't give up.

"Well, he's in his twenties, I guess. I don't know exactly."

Kurt is twenty-three years old. The last thing I wanted to talk about was Kurt. So I changed the subject. I asked Mrs. Snyder how her dog was.

By that time Mom had the salad made. We were going to eat in the kitchen, so Mom had cleared everything off the table and put the green-flowered placemats out. Then she made some iced tea and got out the green cloth napkins. She found a bag of chips in the freezer and emptied them into a bowl and made some Lipton Onion Soup California Dip. Then she went out the back door and snipped a yellow rose, put it in a crystal vase, and placed it in the center of the table. Tyler said once that my mom lives as if she were expecting a photographer from *House Beautiful* to arrive momentarily.

Pretty soon Gregg rang the bell and I let him in. We all sat down at the table and Mom smiled at Gregg. "I made your salad double-sized," she said.

Gregg picked up his fork. "It looks delicious. Thank you."

My mom is really pretty, you know? She's tiny and delicate and fair. Her complexion is light and clear, and her hair is sort of golden, like a halo. Her teeth are real small, but she seems to have so many of them. She has this dazzling smile. So did Francie. Francie looked a lot like Mom.

I bet you thought I was going to say that I look like my dad. Actually, everybody says I look more like my Aunt Marion, Mom's sister. And that doesn't make me too wild with happiness. She's still got pimples, for gods' sake, and she's forty years old! That's my fate. I know it.

The thing I dislike most about Aunt Marion, though, is that

she's generally so abrasive. Tyler says that's probably because of her profession. Aunt Marion's a nurse. Nurses have to get slightly abrasive, or they'll go crazy seeing all that death and misery. It got to be too much for Uncle Phil though. They split up about six years ago, before we moved here. I overheard my mom talking long distance to my grandmother in Cleveland about the divorce, and she said she thought it had something to do with waffles. That's all I know about it.

Aunt Marion's not ugly or anything. I don't mean that. She's just sort of average-looking, I guess. She's taller than Mom, and so am I, but only by a few inches. Aunt Marion and I both have dark hair and slightly protruding upper teeth. My parents took me to see an orthodontist when I was eight or nine. It was my mom's idea. I can remember her saying something about how she didn't want her daughter's smile ruined by buck teeth. But the dentist said there was nothing wrong with my bite and I didn't need braces. That's really quite an amazing thing for an orthodontist to say, when you think about it.

When people say I resemble Aunt Marion, it always surprises me. Except for our teeth and our hair, I can't see that much resemblance. Strange as it seems, I don't know what I look like, and that's the truth. When I was little, back in Van Nuys, I used to think I was quite ugly. That was because the only place I could see myself was in the toaster. I couldn't reach the bathroom mirror, so I used to stare at my reflection a lot in the toaster. It was just the right height, there on the counter. My eyes were really close together and my cheeks puffed out like a chipmunk's. Now, the only place where I look uglier than in the toaster is in the fitting rooms at Mervyn's. I don't know how they do it. Either it's the lights, or they get special mirrors from Transylvania or someplace.

Sometimes I stare at myself in the mirror at home for long

periods of time, trying to figure out what I look like. Gregg told me once that he thought I was beautiful. He said it as a joke, but from the way he blushed after he said it I knew he meant it. And my mom sometimes tells me I'm pretty, but usually in a backhanded way. Just the other day she said, "You've got a really pretty smile, Alfie. You should try to use it more." I said, "Sure, Mom, just give me something to smile about." In our photo albums there's only about three pictures of me smiling, and one of them is because Francie is tickling me. When someone points a camera at me and orders me to smile, I automatically get extremely glum. I just can't smile on command. My mom, however, is going to smile her way through life even if it kills her.

We finished the tuna salad and Mom got out the dessert. The conversation was extremely dull and boring. I must admit that I wasn't much help. I just sat there and ate. That's the trouble with living in a *House Beautiful* setting. It's generally so boring. I mean, Tyler's house looks like *Mad Magazine*, but it's interesting over there. And her parents are normal, at least.

For dessert we had Stella D'Oro cookies and little dishes of raspberry sherbet. Gregg got a double-sized one. As soon as I finished my sherbet I said, "Well, I guess I'd better go do my homework."

"You go ahead, dear," Mom said.

"Yes, we'll do up the dishes," Mrs Snyder added. I don't know what it *is* about her.

Gregg just looked at me with those big, pale blue eyes. "Need any help with your homework?"

Gregg's a senior. When Mom's around, he likes to play big brother. About once a month I have to yell at him to keep his big hands to himself. He's okay though, I guess.

"No thanks, I just have lots of reading to do," I said. Actually, I didn't have any reading to do.

"Well, maybe I'll come by tomorrow."

I was halfway to my room by then. "Well, really Gregg, I've missed a lot of school. I'm going to be really busy for the next couple of days." I wasn't behind at all, of course, but I didn't feel like talking to anybody. I just wanted to be by myself.

"Well," he said, "I'll call you, anyway."

So I sort of groaned and told them all goodnight and went to my room.

My dad didn't come home the next night, either, but he called on the phone. My mom talked to him first. I was in my room, so I couldn't hear all of what she was saying. Not that I didn't try. They didn't talk very long, though. Then Mom called me to the phone. She smiled that troubled, mysterious, other-worldly smile she has. "It's your father. He'd like to speak with you."

I took the phone. "Hi, Daddy."

"Hello, Alfie." He sounded tired. "How's school? Back to the old grind?"

"Oh sure. No problem."

"Say, Alfie . . ."

"Yeah?"

"Alfie, I think we should have a little talk. Uh . . ."

"Where *are* you?"

"Well," his voice dropped. "I'm here in town. I'm, uh, at a motel."

I didn't say anything stupid like, "What the heck are you doing in a *motel?*"

"So how about if I pick you up after school tomorrow? We can go someplace."

"Sure. That'd be okay. On Fridays, though, I have to update the gradebooks for Mr. Burr. I should be done around four or four-thirty."

"I'll pick you up in front of the flagpole at four-thirty then."

"Okay, Daddy. Well, bye." I hung up the phone and said to Mom, "He wants to talk to me."

"I know."

I plunged right in. "What's going on anyway? Why isn't he home?"

My mom took a deep breath. Whenever she takes a deep breath, she stretches her neck way up and her head kind of quivers. I thought for a second she might cry. But she didn't. She just got real busy instead, puttering around, putting the scissors in a drawer, straightening the little stack of notepaper by the phone, turning her back to me.

"He'll explain that to you, honey," she said, her voice quivering slightly.

But I wouldn't give up. "I don't get it, Mom. Why don't *you* explain it to me?"

Mom sat down and put her hand to her forehead and closed her eyes. "We agreed . . . ," she said, shaking her head, "your father and I agreed that since it was his. . . ." Then she broke down and cried and said she couldn't talk about it anymore.

"Oh, Mom!" I whispered, going up to her. "What *is* it? What's *wrong?*"

She just shook her head some more. "Your father will explain it."

She got up from the chair and started toward her room. "I've got to go lie down now, Alfie. I'm sorry."

I sat alone for a long time. I can't remember dreading anything more than I was dreading that little talk with my father, because I knew what he was going to say. They were going to get divorced. I knew that, for sure.

3

I F YOU EVER GET A CHANCE TO LOOK AT ONE
of those relief maps of California, you should
do it. I like looking at maps. Whenever I go
somewhere, I always like to look at the map and picture right
where I am. I just always like to know where I am.

In Van Nuys, after my dad found out he had gotten the job
in Sacramento and that we were going to move, he took me
in the office of the Mobil station where he always got gas and
showed me the relief map of California. It's really amazing.
Most of the state is covered with these blue-green mountains,
but right in the middle is this huge, finger-shaped, light-green
flat part — the San Joaquin Valley. Dad showed me Highway 99 running right through the middle of the valley, from
Bakersfield in the south up to Red Bluff in the north. And he
showed me where the new highway, Highway 5, was going
to be. It's completed now, of course. And then he pointed to
Sacramento. "This is where we're going," he said. "Sure,
it gets hot there, in the summers, but we'll have air condi-
tioning, and there's lots of trees. But best of all, no smog!"

The smog in Van Nuys was very bad for Francie. That was one of the main reasons why we were moving.

Before Francie started getting worse, Dad and I used to take her on little freeway trips around here and there. My mom would usually stay home because she gets carsick a lot. I used to love those trips, looking at all those funky, run-down houses by the side of the road, with backyards like junkyards. Sometimes we'd see those other kinds of houses, too. They were in subdivisions, behind big wooden fences — rows and rows of houses, all the same, and little scrawny trees.

Our new house wasn't in a subdivision, but it wasn't run-down either. Although our backyard borders on the freeway, we don't hear the traffic much because our yard is really long and full of trees and bushes. Our backyard is in two parts. The part near the house has a little lawn and some flowers and a tall hedge. Behind the hedge is the *back* backyard. We don't have any junk cars or rusty old washing machines back there, but we do have a little storage shed and a small chicken coop.

That's the part I like best — the chicken coop. I love to sit out there on the chicken coop roof and watch the world go by. I'm close enough to the freeway to see what the truck drivers and people in their cars look like, and I can wave at them when I feel like it. Sometimes they wave back. It's a funny feeling, waving to people you don't know and won't ever see again. Your paths may only touch for a second, but still you're part of each other's lives forever.

I can see clear across the highway from up there, and all the way to the auto wrecking yard about half a mile up the road. The people right across the road don't have a clothes dryer I guess, because they always have clothes on their line. I love seeing their sheets and towels and pants and little stuff

I can't make out, probably socks and underwear, flapping in the breeze.

We have eucalyptus trees, too, three of them by the back fence. There's nothing I like better than sitting out there all alone on the chicken coop under the eucalyptus trees in the late afternoon and smelling that lovely eucalyptus smell. It's such a nostalgic odor. It makes me think of Gregg and that very first summer we spent together when I was just thirteen.

We met because of his little dog, Skipper. I was washing my hair in the kitchen sink the second morning we were here, still in my stockinged feet, when I saw this cute little dog tearing across the street; it almost got hit by a car. Then it came sniffing around our bushes and kind of crying. I put a towel on my head and went out to see it. Scratched on its collar was "If found, please call" and a phone number. It was a real little dog, and cute, so I brought it in the house for Francie to pet. Francie used to like dogs, but not those real large ones. So I held him in my arms and let her pet him for a while. We gave him a drink, and he was so thirsty that we decided he must have been lost for a long time. I put him out in our side yard so he wouldn't jump all over Francie while I was calling the number on his collar. But before I finished dialing the number, the crazy dog jumped over the fence and started running down the street. Francie was watching out the window. "He escaped!" she screamed. "Hurry, Alfie! Go get him!"

I banged down the receiver and took off after him. What a chase! He kept crisscrossing over people's lawns and flower beds and through sprinklers until he had me completely out of breath. A couple of times I almost grabbed him, but he thought I was playing a game I guess, because he just wouldn't let me get hold of him.

Finally he went up on the porch of this little green house

with white shutters. I snuck up from around the side and snatched him right up. He started licking my face and neck and struggling like anything, getting his muddy paws all over me. I managed to carry him all the way home, but I was a real mess when I got there.

This time I got a piece of rope and tied him to the fence while I called. Gregg answered the phone. I told him I had his little dog and gave him our address. He said he'd be right over.

The first words Gregg said to me when he got here were, "Brother! What happened to *you?*"

I looked down at myself. I still hadn't put on my shoes, and my white socks were torn and muddy. My blouse was hanging out of my jeans and covered with muddy paw prints, and my hair, which I never had combed, was sticking out every which-way. I explained that it was all that little dog's fault. I told Gregg how he had escaped from our yard and how I had had to chase him all over the neighborhood.

"Where did you finally catch him?" Gregg asked, kind of suspiciously.

"At a little green house, down that way," I pointed. Gregg looked at me and started laughing. "You know something? That's where he *lives.* That's our house. You rescued him from his own house!"

Gregg started coming over regularly after that, especially after our mothers met at church. He liked me from the start, and I actually didn't mind him too much. Francie was the one who really liked him, though. He was so nice to her. He used to kid her about his being her boyfriend. But he was always nice about it. He wasn't making fun of her or anything. Lots of times he would bring her little presents, nothing much, maybe a flower or a cupcake his mother had baked or something like that. Actually, when I think about it now, that's probably the reason I didn't mind so much that he was always hanging around here. The three of us used to have lots of fun together.

One time Francie asked me real seriously if I *liked* Gregg. I told her sure, I guess I liked him.

"No," she said, blushing. "I mean do you *really* like him? Do you want to marry him?" she whispered.

"Marry him?" I said. "Oh, no. He's just not my type, honey."

The fact is, though, that I did have a wild crush on him for about two weeks after we first met, but then suddenly it was over. I remember telling him he could still come over if he wanted, but we'd just be *friends,* if he knew what I meant. Only poor Gregg can't ever seem to forget those first two weeks.

After I told Francie that Gregg was not for me, she practically glowed. Just to make her feel even better, I added, "Besides, Francie, I thought he was *your* boyfriend!" Boy, her smile was so big! I don't know what to think about all that now. It was harmless, I guess, and it sure made Francie happy. But it was kind of pathetic, too, in a way.

Just the other day Gregg reminded me of something that the three of us did one afternoon. It seems so long ago now. It was just a few weeks after we had moved in, and my mom and Aunt Marion were shopping for drapes in San Francisco and my dad was at work, so I was left in charge of Francie. It was about ten in the morning and Gregg and I were up on the roof and Francie was sitting down below in her wheelchair. It was pretty hard getting her back there, since there's no path or anything, but it wasn't impossible. When Gregg was here, we just carried her — wheelchair and all. On this particular morning she was being extra quiet down there, not chattering away like she usually did. Finally I called down to her and asked her what she was thinking.

"I'm just talking to Jesus," she said, in her sincere way. She used to talk to Jesus a lot. Like my mom.

Anyway, when Francie said she had been talking to Jesus, Gregg asked, real kindly, "What about, Francie?"

She closed her eyes. "Oh, I was just telling Him that I sure wished I could go up there on the roof and see the trucks and the automobile graveyard and the neighbor's clothesline and stuff."

I jumped down when she said that. "Let's go do something else," I said. "Let's go look around in the shed."

The lady who sold us this place didn't want to be bothered cleaning out all the junk in the garage and shed, so it all just came with the house. My mom wanted to call somebody to haul it all away, but Dad said that he wanted to look through it first. Dad always *says* stuff like that, but he never does it. My mom keeps reminding him about it all the time, but he still doesn't do anything about it.

Well, we put Francie in the doorway of the shed where she could watch us, and Gregg and I went in and started rummaging around. Gregg found this old lampshade and made Francie laugh by putting it on his head and doing a little dance. Then I opened this heavy cardboard carton and found something really interesting.

"Hey Gregg, look!" I hauled up a long rope and all this stuff that was attached to it.

"What is it?"

"I think it's a block and tackle. I read an article in the *World Book* about it one time. Yep," I finally decided, "that's what it is, all right."

Gregg made his way over to my side, brushing spider webs

from his arms. Gregg's not fat, exactly, but he's got one of those bodies where you can't tell where his muscles are. Oh, he's pretty strong, and his arms are really solid, but they're sort of round. His blond hair was falling down all over his eyes. Since then, he goes and gets his hair styled. It sounds dumb, but I must admit it has improved his looks. And he's grown a lot, too. He's over six feet tall now. But his face hasn't changed much. It's still really simple and open. You know what I mean? His face is sort of like a big, friendly white frying pan, and his eyes are like two big blue fried eggs.

"Are you sure it's a block and tackle?" he asked.

"Of course. What else? Come on. I've got an idea."

We went in the house then and brought the block and tackle in with us. Even though it was a little early for Francie's late morning bed rest, we put her down anyway. I didn't want her to hear us talking and get her hopes up for nothing. I found the article in the *World Book* and showed it to Gregg. "What do you think?" I asked softly. "Can we get her up there?"

"Well, let's see." He read the article out loud a few times, and I held up the little pulley things, matching them to the diagrams in the book. "Gee," he said, "I don't know."

But I was really excited. "Listen, Gregg, we can try it and see if it works while she's resting. You know, we can haul up the empty wheelchair."

The whole thing was really pretty easy. We just followed the diagrams and tied some ropes onto the tree and the chair and we were hauling the thing up and down in no time.

After Francie's rest time, I said to her, "How would you like to have a picnic out in back for lunch?"

"Oh, could we?" God, it was really fun doing stuff for Francie. She got such a big kick out of everything.

After we got her out in the back again, I climbed up on the roof and said, "How about lunch in the penthouse?"

30

"What's that?"

"Up here, you dope."

Gregg had all the ropes attached again, and I was up on the roof, ready to bring her in for a landing.

Boy, that little kid was sure gutsy. She was really scared as she went up. She kept making little muffled screaming noises, but we made it just fine.

She loved it up there. She just kept saying, "Thank you, thank you."

But while Francie was up there enjoying the view, I was starting to worry about the consequences. My mom and dad were not going to take to that idea at all. I knew that without even asking. And Francie would probably want to be up there all the time now. But that's where I was wrong. When we finally got her back down, she was shaking all over.

"Well, was that fun?" I asked as we were untying the ropes.

"Oh, y-yes! But I d-don't want to ever do it again! I'm really glad I saw it, Alfie, but it's just too scary!"

That was sure a relief. "Well then, honey," I said, "no use worrying Mommy and Daddy about it, okay? See, they might not like the idea of you being up there at all, even though we know it was perfectly safe, but you know how they are. So let's just not mention. . . ."

"Sure, Alfie. That's okay."

After Francie was in bed that night, she squeezed my hand and whispered, "See, Alfie, Jesus really does answer my prayers!"

Helping Jesus answer Francie's prayers was a little habit of mine. I have to mention one other time that I did it, because it gets sort of important later on. It happened one afternoon on the day before Francie's seventh birthday, back in Van Nuys. My mom was working out in her flower beds and Francie and I were playing Chutes and Ladders in her room.

31

She was cheating a little, as usual. Francie really liked to win when we played games, and sometimes she resorted to some pretty weird ways of doing it. One of her favorites was asking me to go get her a handkerchief or something, then while I was out of the room, she'd rearrange pieces and stuff like that. Sometimes I called her on it, sometimes I didn't.

Anyway, I had already bought her birthday present. It was a really nice fake silver crucifix on a chain that I had found in a Salvation Army store. I say it was real nice because it wasn't just a plain cross. This was one of those big ones, and it had an actual representation of Jesus on it, nailed to the cross. You could even see the little spikes going through his hands. I remember it cost $2.59. I was wearing it under my T-shirt, sort of breaking it in for her.

Well, I was planning to go outside and roller-skate as soon as Mom came back in. But Francie didn't want me to go and leave her. She started whining about it, saying things like "Don't go, Alfie! You *never* like to play with me! If you couldn't go out and roller-skate, I'd stay in with you!" Then she started crying.

"Hey, cut it out now," I said, slightly annoyed.

She was really crying now. "How come I've prayed and prayed to get well, and Jesus doesn't even hear me?"

"Oh, come on, Francie."

"I don't think He even hears me!"

"Of course He hears you! But you've got to trust Him and have faith. He knows what's best."

"Okay then," she pouted, "I'm going to pray one more time then. I'll ask Him if He really hears me. I'll ask Him for a sign." Then she closed her eyes real tight and started to pray.

And that's when this really strange thing happened to me.

I've thought about it a million times since then, and I've never been able to forget it. What happened was that the figure of Jesus appeared to me, right there in my head. He looked the way He always did — just like the illustration of Him in this book Mom had given me called *Old and New Testament Bible Stories for Children*. He was standing there, all in white, arms outstretched. Obviously, He wanted me to do something.

Quickly and without even thinking, I undid the clasp on Francie's birthday crucifix and placed it gently in her lap while she was praying there, eyes clamped shut. Then I turned and walked quietly away from her.

A moment later she was shrieking, "Alfie! Look!" She was simply ecstatic. "Look!" She held up the crucifix. "He heard me! See! He heard me!"

My heart was thumping like mad. It was like a miracle for me, too. "Oh, Francie! That's really wonderful!"

I'd never seen her so excited. "Call Mommy, Alfie! Hurry!"

That's when I got scared. I looked to Jesus for some advice, but He was no longer there. I knew Mom would ask me what I knew about this miraculous occurrence, and I would either have to lie to her or tell Francie the truth.

"That's really wonderful, honey," I said, "but you know something? I don't think Jesus wants you to show this to anybody."

"How come?"

"Well, because it might make other people feel bad. You know, the ones who haven't gotten any sign yet?"

"But I have to show it to Mom!"

"Oh, no, honey! Not even Mom! *Especially* Mom! Whenever Jesus leaves a sign, He means for it to be private." Then I added the clincher. "It says so in the Bible."

"But Mom will see it!"

"Not if we keep it hidden! And only take it out when we're alone."

"Well," she asked hesitantly, "where could we keep it?"

My mind was racing. I remembered a secret hiding place I'd discovered some time ago. "I know just the place."

I went over to her closet and removed the little bottom drawer of her built-in dresser. It was full to the top with games and scraps of paper, and it was really hard to pull out. "Right here, Francie," I said. "Under here. See?"

"Wait!" she exclaimed. "Find a little box for it, okay? Put it in a box first."

I knew Mom would be back in the house in a few minutes, so I didn't have much time. The only box I could find was an empty Jell-O box I found in the garbage. "This is great!" I told Francie. "No one will ever suspect it's in here!"

She didn't argue with me. If you handled Francie right, you could get away with murder. You could talk her into anything — even hiding a miraculous crucifix in a cherry Jell-O box.

As far as I know, Francie was true to her word. She never mentioned that crucifix to anyone. And often, during our remaining months in Van Nuys, whenever we were alone together in her room and she would ask me, I'd remove the bottom drawer of her dresser and get it out for her. It was a great comfort to her.

One time my mom came into the room unexpectedly just as I was about to hand the crucifix to Francie. The bottom drawer was already out and sitting on the floor.

"Cleaning out some drawers, girls?"

I quickly clutched the crucifix in my hands and nodded. "Uh-huh."

"That's nice," Mom smiled, as she put the clean sheets away.

Several months later, in the confusion of moving day, we forgot the crucifix. I forgot the crucifix, I mean. It was my fault. Francie had whispered to me, reminding me, but the opportunity to get it out never came. And in the end, I simply forgot it.

As soon as we were alone in our house in Sacramento, Francie called me over to her. "We've got to find a new hiding place," she whispered.

My heart sank. "Oh, Francie! I'm sorry! I forgot to get it! It's still at the old house!"

I thought she'd be crushed, but instead she only smiled and patted my hand. "That's okay, Alfie," she said, with typical childlike faith. "Don't feel bad. Jesus will bring it to me."

Well, I was just a thirteen-year-old kid, but somehow I knew that Jesus Christ — although He could make the lame to walk and cause the blind to see — simply could not deliver a crucifix from Van Nuys to Sacramento.

4

ON FRIDAY AFTERNOON I FINISHED GET-
ting the gradebooks up to date for Mr.
Burr and went out to meet my dad by
the flagpole a little before four-thirty. He was early, too. He
drives this old blue Mercedes diesel that he bought from some
guy he works with. He even has a special license plate for it.
It's got the letters *MB* for Mercedes Benz, and then Dad's ini-
tials. The license plate was Mom's idea. The plate that was
on the car when he got it had the number *666* in it. And those
sixes made Mom nervous, because the number *666* is the Mark
of the Beast. In the days of the Antichrist, the number *666* is
going to be on people's foreheads, or their right hands, according to the Bible and according to my mom. That's either
before or after the unbelievers have been destroyed in the lake
of fire and the faithful have been caught up in the sky with
Jesus. I never can get that part straight.

My dad's Mercedes is so old it's practically an antique. Men
are always yelling out their car windows at him at stop lights,
shouting things like, "Nice car you got there!" "What year is

that baby?" "Hey, you want to sell that thing?" My dad loves
it when they do that. He doesn't like to talk about real stuff
much, but he always likes to talk to strangers about his car.

Dad leaned over and opened the passenger door for me.
"Hi, Alfie." He looked pretty haggard.

"Hi, Dad."

"Hot fudge sundae?"

"Uh, sure. I guess." A hot fudge sundae meant we were
going to Denny's. That's where we always used to go with
Francie, and I really didn't feel like going there right then.
But I couldn't explain all that to my dad. We'd usually go
out to dinner at Denny's on Thursday nights, if my dad was
in town and if Francie felt well enough to go. They were always nice to us there, even though her wheelchair kind of got
in the way.

Dad started chattering as soon as I got in the car. He has
this nervous chatter; whenever he talks about nothing, he does
it real fast. He had this ashtray on the seat of the car and he
told me it was from the motel he was staying at. He made me
look at it. It had the name of the motel on it. It was nothing
spectacular.

He told me that one of his work friends, Bill Brazier, collected ashtrays from motels and that he would probably be
overjoyed at my dad's great find.

"Really?" I said.

"Oh, definitely! Now look at the phone number," he in-
structed.

"The phone number?"

"Yes. Don't you see?" He took his eyes off the road for
a second and pointed to something on the ashtray. "See those
letters there? The *GL?* That stands for Gladstone. That's an
old phone number, Alfie. Maybe even prewar! Bill's gonna

37

love it. He's got several hundred of them, you know. From all over!'' Dad looked at me sideways and added, ''He ashes for them everywhere he goes.''

''That's amazing,'' I said, ignoring the pun. I ignore his, and he ignores mine.

Then he spent the rest of the time on the way to Denny's telling me about Bill Brazier's fabulous ashtray collection. He even had one from a place called Rick's American Cafe. But it wasn't from Casablanca. It was from Baltimore or somewhere.

I knew it was a mistake — going to Denny's — as soon as we walked in and I saw Lois. She's this real nice old waitress who always talked directly to Francie, like she was an actual person and not some inanimate object or something. Lots of times when we were out with Francie, waitresses would ask my mother what Francie wanted, as if Francie wasn't even there. That always made me really mad.

The hostess waved us over to a table in back, and Lois came right over with her coffee pot and poured some for Dad. ''Well, where's the rest of the family today?''

My heart made a big jolt and I looked up at Dad. You'd think he'd be ready for that question. After all, he was the one who wanted to come here. But he wasn't ready at all. He looked like he'd just been hit by a brick. His face clouded over and his eyes suddenly got all red and watery. I couldn't stand to see him like that. Then he got out his handkerchief and took off his glasses, real slowly. Well, poor Lois was just standing there all this time, looking from Dad to me and then to Dad again. Pretty soon she caught on. ''Oh,'' she said quietly. ''Something bad, huh?''

Dad still didn't say anything.

''She died last Friday.'' That was me. I said, ''She died last Friday,'' and then I started to cry. God, it was awful.

38

Old Lois said a few more words — I don't know what she said — and then she went away and came back with some water.

My dad was all pulled together by then. "Let's have one of your special hot fudge sundaes for the young lady."

"One hot fudge sundae."

"Something to drink, Alfie? A Coke, maybe?"

I nodded, still sniffing. I hate public scenes.

"And a large Coke, please," Dad cleared his throat. "I'll just have the coffee for now."

We didn't say anything for quite a while. Dad kept stirring his coffee and sipping a little and then stirring it again. Finally he put the spoon down on his napkin and put his fingers to his temple. "Alfie, this probably won't come as a big surprise to you, but your mother and I have decided to end our marriage."

Just as he said that, Lois appeared with my Coke and sundae. She had heard every word. I could tell it really flustered her. At first she put the Coke in front of my dad. Then she realized her mistake and moved it in front of me. I just wanted to fall through the floor. I bet she did, too.

Hot fudge sundaes always look good to me. But that one sure didn't. I took a little tentative bite, because I didn't know what else to do, and then I wondered if I was going to get sick.

My dad was sort of looking off into space and sliding his fingers around his hairline. I just waited.

"We haven't had a real marriage for years. I guess you've sensed that — haven't you, Alfie? She's changed, Alfie. She's not the same person I married."

I didn't know what to say. I just sat there feeling sick, watching my hot fudge sundae melt.

"I mean, hell, we used to go to church together on Sundays. I was willing to go along with it that far, at least. But now, you know, Alfie — I suppose Francie has had a great deal to do with it — but she's really gone overboard on this religious thing.'' He smiled, but it was not exactly a smile. ''Sometimes I think she talks to Jesus more than she talks to me. And that's a fact.''

I nodded. ''Yeah,'' I said softly.

My dad pushed his coffee cup to one side and lit a cigarette. ''And now, with Francie gone, there's no reason. . . .''

He didn't finish his sentence. I was thinking about what he had just said though — *with Francie gone there's no reason* — and I blurted out, ''Well, what about me? I'm still here, for gods' sake!''

That was a stupid thing to say, but my feelings were really hurt. It was like they stayed together for Francie but that I wasn't worth staying together for, or something. But it was stupid and I shouldn't have said it.

''Well, Alfie, that's a little different situation. You're . . .'' he paused, shaking his head.

''Oh, I know, Dad,'' I said finally. ''I'm sorry. I know it's different. I don't know what's the matter with me.''

My hot fudge sundae was melting all over now, running down the sides of the dish. I pushed it to one side. Pretty soon Lois came by and saw it there. She just looked at me a second and raised her eyebrows a little. Then she took it away. That made me start crying all over again. There are some really nice, understanding people in this world, you know?

I took a couple of sips of Coke and tried to calm down. ''So, what happens to me, then?''

''What do you mean, Alfie?'' God, I hated it when my dad was like that. When he makes you spell everything out for him.

40

"You know what I mean! What's going to happen to me?"

"Like where will you live, and things like that?"

I just looked at him. I was so mad, I wouldn't even nod.

"That'll be up to you, mostly."

"You mean I can move away and live by myself?" Sometimes I can be really pretty snotty.

"Of course not, Alfie!" he said stiffly. "Now don't get difficult. I mean you can stay with either your mother or me." His voice softened. "Anyway, you'll be going off to college before you know it. Here it is almost summer, and your senior year will go by plenty fast."

Lois came by again and refilled his coffee cup. I couldn't stand to look at her. Suddenly I wished I was *her* kid. She probably had a very nice husband. They probably got along really well.

My dad smiled at Lois. "Thanks," he said. Then he looked across the booth at me again. "Speaking of college, how were your PSAT scores, anyway? We haven't had a chance to talk about that."

"Huh?"

"Your PSAT scores. How were they?"

"Oh, pretty good." I blew my nose. Actually, I had gotten the second highest in the school.

"How good?"

"Mr. Coombs said I got the second highest in the school."

"That's good, baby!" Once in a great while my dad calls me baby. Just then some guy walked by carrying a newspaper. Dad snapped his fingers and stood up suddenly. "Oh, listen Alfie," he said, "excuse me for a sec, will you? I want to get a paper before they're all sold out. I was too late last night, and there's nothing to do in that damn motel."

Then he was gone. My dad's a great newspaper reader. When he's out of town, we have to save them all in a nice orderly pile. *At least we won't have to do that anymore,* I thought, and the tears came back in my eyes.

I sat there drinking my Coke and trying to think about something besides divorce. *Anything* but divorce. I thought about my PSAT scores, and then I thought about Victor Beauchamp. Victor Beauchamp got the *highest* grade in the school on the PSAT. Talk about brains. And I like the way he looks, too. I like guys who look complicated and cynical and are not *smiling* all the time. Like Kurt. Kurt and Victor are a lot alike.

After that little exchange with Victor about Fred Astaire, I made a point of asking Tyler about him. "What's the deal, anyway?" I asked. "How did you and Victor get so friendly?"

She laughed. "Ah, you mean my twin!"

"Huh?"

"We were born on the same day. Our mothers met in the hospital. They were roommates after Victor and I were born. And it was really neat, because our fathers already knew each other. That was back when my dad worked on the paper."

"So that's it."

"Our mothers had us married off before our first diaper change," Tyler smiled. "We practically grew up together."

"So when's the wedding?"

"Oh, come on, Alfie. He's just a good friend."

"What's wrong with him, anyway? Why does he seem so, oh, aloof all the time?"

"Oh, he is pretty weird, I suppose; at least he seems that way, until you get to know him. For one thing, he's so smart. And then, he's an only child and all that. He's just super-sensitive, that's all."

Tyler brightened suddenly. "Hey, *you're* not interested in him, are you?" She got this amazed look on her face. "Come to think of it, you two — hmm. *Veerry interesting!* I'll see what I can do."

"Tyler! If you say anything to him about me, I'll. . . ."

Just as I was thinking about the way Tyler had looked when I said that to her, my dad came back with his newspaper and slid back into his seat.

"Let's see," he said. "Where were we? How about college? Do you have any ideas where you'd like to go?"

It was obvious he had said all he was going to about the divorce.

"Oh, not really." I had been looking over some catalogues in Mr. Coombs's office the other day and noticed they had some stuff there from Caltech. There was a little brochure telling about their math and science classes, with pictures of the students and campus. One picture showed a girl with some books under her arm. The caption underneath said, "What's a nice girl like you doing in a place like this?" Boy, I'd *love* to go there!

"Where do you think you'd like to go?"

"Oh, I don't know. Caltech sounds sort of nice, if we can afford it. And if I can get in."

That seemed okay with my dad. Just then his digital watch beeped and he checked the time. "There's no need for any hurried decisions. You and your mother getting on okay?"

"Well, so far. But it's going to be hard for me if she starts. . . ."

"Well," he interrupted, "let's just see how it goes."

He started to get up then, and so did I, but then he sort of sat down again, with his leg sticking in the aisle. "Oh, there is one more thing."

"Yeah?"

"I'm supposed to make it clear to you that this . . . this divorce business is *my* idea. Your mother. . . ."

43

"I know, Dad," I interrupted. "That's okay. I understand."

He reached over for my hand and we looked at each other. He nodded and squeezed my fingers in the palm of his hand. "Thanks, Alfie." There was a little catch in his voice. He leaned over and kissed me on the forehead. "You're a good girl."

Dad drove me home then and stopped the car in front of our house. He kept the motor running though. "I'll keep in touch," he said. "You have my number at the motel?"

"Uh-huh."

"Remember you can get me at the office, too, if you need to. They always know where I am."

"Okay."

"And Alfie, I'm really sorry about all this."

And then I said something really weird. It was risky, but I knew it wouldn't be lost on my dad. "Oh, well," I said, "maybe it's just God's will."

My words seem to hang in the air. Dad looked at me for a long time. Finally, he smiled — a really slow, sad smile. "Alfie," he said, "you're okay. You know it? You're really okay."

I quickly brushed away a few tears. "You're okay, too, Daddy," I said.

I smelled the homemade chili as soon as I opened the front door. Mom didn't like chili that much, so I knew she was making it especially for me.

I went right to the kitchen and found her there washing a head of lettuce. When she saw me come in, she shook her hands dry and then reached for a towel.

"Hi, Mom," I said, not quite knowing what to expect.

44

She came up to me without a word and we hugged each other for a long time. I was thinking, as I was standing there, how I just couldn't picture her as a divorced woman.

"Making chili, huh?" I said finally, trying to keep my voice steady.

She took a handkerchief out of her apron pocket and blew her nose and wiped her eyes. "Yes," she nodded, but she couldn't control her quivering lips.

"Please don't cry, Mom," I said desperately, starting to cry myself, and hating it. And for a few moments the only sounds in the kitchen were the humming of the refrigerator and me and Mom crying.

I couldn't stand it. I knew I had to say something. What finally came out was, "Gee, Mom, this is just like some soap opera, huh?"

I don't think my mom will ever get used to some of the things I say. After all these years, I still seem to surprise her. When I said that about a soap opera, she looked for a moment like I had just said something in ancient Greek.

And then she did something really typical. She turned very thoughtful and wise. She was taking my bad joke seriously. "Yes," she nodded, as if she had just seen the light. "I guess it *is* like a soap opera at that, isn't it?"

I realized again how far apart we really were. And strange as it seems, it only made me love her more.

"Oh, Mom," I cried, shaking my head, "what are we going to do?"

"Let's go sit down, Alfie," she said, suddenly in control.

I followed her into the den and noticed she had our photo albums spread out on the coffee table in there. She sat down on the couch and I collapsed in a chair.

"I've been looking through these pictures while you were . . . were with your father this afternoon," she said. Suddenly she buried her face in her arms and started to sob again.

"Oh, Mom!" I instinctively went over to her and put my arms around her. Some of the loose album pages fell on the floor as I brushed past them. I just gazed at them and waited for my mom to stop crying. I didn't know what to say.

After a few minutes she calmed down again and attempted a weak smile. "Well," she said, "I have talked to the Lord about it, and it seems I'm to make the best of it."

I nodded. I had been wondering when she would bring the Lord into the conversation.

We separated then and she leaned over and picked up a loose page from the floor. It contained several pictures of her and Dad leaving for their honeymoon. She quickly put it aside and took up one of the albums. She started turning the pages. "Look, honey," she said, making an attempt at normal conversation. "That's when we first brought you home from the hospital."

I had seen those pictures a hundred times, but now I seemed to be looking at them through her eyes.

"Look at you on the pony." She flipped more pages. My first day in kindergarten, our house in Van Nuys, and then a picture of Francie, a tiny baby in Dad's arms, and me standing proudly at his side.

Now Mom turned the pages more slowly. Francie on a blanket, Francie on the couch, Francie being held — but never Francie standing. Finally, Francie strapped in a tiny stroller.

Stuck between the pages of the album, not pasted in, was a slightly overexposed snapshot of Dr. Amos that Francie had taken with her very first camera. He is standing by his office window, with the sunlight streaming in. The picture was not pasted in because he signed it on the back for her: "To Francie, one of my very special friends. Love from Dr. Amos."

Dr. Amos's 'very special friends' were children like Francie, afflicted with congenital muscular diseases.

Mom looked at the picture of Dr. Amos for a minute and then stuck it back between the pages.

"I really and truly tried my best to make the marriage work," Mom said quietly.

The sincerity of that statement went right to my heart. "I know, Mom. It's nobody's fault."

She sighed. "Your father says I've changed. He says. . . ." She closed her eyes and rocked slowly back and forth. "Alfie," she said, almost pleading with me, "the Lord is the only one who gives me peace. I . . . I can't. . . ."

"It's okay, Mom. It's okay." I wished there were some way I could let her know that I really understood.

We didn't talk for a few minutes. I could hear the clock ticking in the hallway.

Then, after a few false starts, my mom said in a tremulous voice, "Did you and your father discuss at all your future living arrangements?"

I looked up. "Well, not really. I guess I'm just staying here."

"And that's all right with you?"

"Well, sure."

She let out a deep sigh of relief. "Oh, Alfie, I was so worried about that. You and your father are so close, I was afraid you might not. . . ." She reached over and hugged me. Now we were both crying again.

"You know, honey, you always seemed so — oh, I don't know — so self-sufficient, somehow."

I couldn't see her face because her chin was on my shoulder. "But I'm beginning to realize now that for these past eleven years, Francie was at the center of — I mean, I think I've neglected. . . ."

"Oh, no!" I interrupted. "No, you haven't."

She grabbed my shoulders and looked directly into my eyes. "Well, if I have, I want to tell you now that I'm sorry. And I'm going to really try to understand you better. I know that we're very different, you and I, and. . . ."

"Hey Mom," I said gently, "I think the chili's ready. Let's go have some, huh?"

5

AFTER WE HAD DINNER, MY MOM DID A FEW things in the kitchen and then told me she had a headache and was going to bed. I went to my room and turned off the light, but I couldn't get to sleep. I tried thinking up some new acne cures, but that didn't help. I'm getting to be a regular insomniac. So I got up and went and watched TV for a while. There was a light on in Mom's room, but I guess she didn't hear me, because she didn't come out or anything.

The program I started with was on our educational channel. It was about the food chain, and it showed how the whole design of nature is a precarious balance of plants, insects and animals, a balance between stalking and attacking prey on the one hand and being stalked and attacked on the other. Insects and animals attack and kill each other as a way of life, and often in cruel and ingenious ways. Out there, in the oceans and deserts and meadows and forests, it is indeed a cruel and gruesome world.

For some perverse reason, it made me think of my mom's favorite song. She's been going around the house humming it for years. It's the one Ethel Waters sings, about God having his eye on every sparrow: "His eye is on the sparrow and I know he's watching me." Well, we had this bird's nest up in our porch roof back in Van Nuys, and every spring the little baby birds would keep falling out of the nest and dying on our bricks. They didn't have any feathers yet, and they were a sort of a purple color. After a day out in the sun, they would get all shriveled up, like jerky. One day my dad happened to mention that they were sparrows, and that really confused me. *It couldn't be,* I thought, *because God's eye is on the sparrow.* I thought about asking my mom about it, but I didn't, because I had a sneaky feeling she would think I was just trying to cause trouble. One day I did ask her, though. We had just had an argument about something else and I was mad at her. So when she started singing her favorite song, I said, "Oh yeah? Well how come if God's eye is on the sparrow, they keep dying on our bricks?"

My mom took me by the hand and sat me down beside her. Then she told me something about how the Bible didn't say that God *took care* of the sparrows. It said He only *watched* them, and He *knew* when harm came to any one of them.

I said, "Well, I think that's terrible. That doesn't help the sparrows much."

"No," she said, nodding her head and looking thoughtful, "but it does show that God cares." I couldn't understand how God could care but still not do anything about it. It didn't make any sense to me at all.

Well, the announcer broke in right in the middle of the food chain program and all of a sudden it was "pledge night." They had a bunch of self-conscious looking people sitting at some phones, and the announcer said that if we wished to continue having such fine programming on educational TV, we should do our part and send in our checks and pledges.

I knew that was going to go on for about ten minutes, so I switched to the religious channel and tuned in for a while on Jim and Tammy Bakker and the PTL Club. PTL stands either for Praise the Lord or People That Love — I don't know which. Anyway, old Jim and Tammy were standing over this huge bin sort of thing that was chock-full of letters. Jim poured some oil — not much, just a little — over the letters, saying that he was anointing them, just like it said in the Bible. The letters were all prayer requests that his listeners had sent in. Then some church elders came up and they all joined hands while Jim prayed. I can't remember his exact words, but he had his eyes closed real tight and he was asking the Lord, in the name of *Je*sus, to please grant the requests in the bin. In the background there were some people sitting at telephones, taking pledges for money to keep Jim Bakker and the PTL Club on the air. Suddenly the program was almost over. This fat guy they call Uncle Henry was giving the address where you could send your money. The PTL Club was in financial crisis. They had lots of bills to pay (TV time is not cheap) and unless God sent them a miracle, they might have to go off the air. He said the counselors would be standing by even after the program was off the air. And remember, the good thing about sending money to help God was that usually God saw that you were repaid, sometimes even tenfold.

I switched back to the food chain program and watched a coyote tackle a little lame deer that couldn't keep up with the rest. The narrator explained that was nature's way of keeping the herd strong and fit.

When it was over, I thought about those two programs for a long time, and about that old saying, "You pays your money and you takes your choice."

I didn't feel like watching any more television after that. I sort of felt like calling up my dad. But it was pretty late and

I wasn't sure if he'd still be up. I wondered if he had his jogging stuff at the motel. My dad goes jogging about every night — at least he used to — right after he gets home from work. He always invited me along. It's funny about jogging. I mean, I hate the thought of it, but I'm happy once I'm out there. My dad's pretty skinny and he runs pretty fast for me, but I can usually keep up. Except when we get to old Cardiac Hill, of course. That's when I usually start breathing hard, and I have to slow down to a walk.

Gee, maybe we could still do that. Go jogging, I mean. Maybe he could come over and pick me up in the car and we could go jog in the park or something. I'd really like that.

We haven't been out jogging together for weeks. Actually, I think the last time we went was the afternoon he told me about the creation trial.

I had been telling him how I needed a project for a class I'm taking, and he suggested the trial.

"What's it about?" I asked. "Who's suing *who?*"

"Well, this group in San Diego — the Creation–Science Research Center — is suing the State Department of Education. They want to have creation taught along with evolution in science classes."

"Well," I said, considering, "that seems fair."

"Think so? There's been a lot of disagreement about that. The arguments on both sides should be very interesting."

He thought about it for a few minutes. "If you do decide to take it on as a project though, you'd have to miss school, of course, in order to attend the trial. How would your MGM teacher feel about that?"

"He probably wouldn't mind. They excuse kids for everything in that class." I had to quit talking for a minute to catch my breath. Then I said, "Thanks for the suggestion, Daddy.

You know, that sounds like it'd be a really great MGM project. Except for missing school," I grinned.

MGM is this really dumb thing we have at my school. When you're in elementary or maybe even in middle school, if the teacher recommends you, you can take this test. I guess it's an IQ test, actually. If you get above a certain grade, they call you an MGM, or Mentally Gifted Minor. I don't know who thought that up. Anyway, then you get to go on all kinds of special trips and stuff, and all the other kids get jealous and mad. And you can take special classes like the one I'm in now, where you just get special counseling and do projects and things. The reason I think it's dumb is because some of the kids act really terrible on the trips, especially in the lower grades, and they don't even care about what they're going to see. The sad part is that some of the kids that didn't get in MGM would probably be really interested and would want to go. And I know for a fact that some kids that didn't get in MGM are definitely smarter in some ways than the kids that did. I don't think one little test is going to show who's smarter than whom. From what I've heard about Einstein and Thomas Edison and people like that, they probably wouldn't have made it into MGM. I read in the *World Book* once that Thomas Edison's teacher thought he was "addled." I think what they should do is tell *all* the kids when there's a trip coming up, to the nuclear power plant or the shoelace factory or whatever, then any kid who does a paper or a book report on the subject can go.

The best thing that happened in my MGM class was that I met Tyler there. We really didn't start talking to each other much until one day a couple of weeks after the class started. It was around the end of October, last year, because we were meeting in the Student Activities room and the Pep Rally

Committee had been making posters for the Halloween dance; they had left their paste and paints and stuff all over the place.

There were three or four of us sitting around a table discussing our career goals when Tyler swatted this big green fly with her gym sock. She didn't kill it, she only dazed it. It fell on the table, and started buzzing and whirling around in circles. I don't know what made me do it, but I picked up a bottle of silver glitter that the Pep Rally Committee had left on the table, and I sprinkled it on the fly. Then I sort of clapped my hands and went, "Yeah, yeah — disco fly!"

It broke old Tyler up. I thought she was going to fall on the floor laughing. I usually speak pretty softly, and I think she was the only one who heard what I said, because the other kids were just watching her cracking up, not knowing what was going on. Pretty soon Mr. Schlitz came running over to join the action. He's also the German teacher and speaks with a pretty heavy accent. Tyler wants to be an actress and she's really good at imitating people. She's got Mr. Schlitz down pat.

Tyler and I talked the entire rest of the period. She told me she had seen me before, eating lunch with Bonnie and Marcie. I told her I knew them from church.

"Ah," she said, "a couple of Bible-bunnies, huh?"

I guess I looked kind of shocked, because she smiled sort of apologetically and said she really didn't mean it as an insult.

The thing I like best about Tyler is her complete independence. I mean, she knows practically everybody in the school, but lots of times you see her just walking along happily all by herself, her bushy auburn hair shining almost red in the sun. I walk along by myself lots of times, too, but I'm always sort of embarrassed about it, although I try not to look like it and I hate to admit it.

Tyler and I talked a little about our families that first day. She has two brothers: Jerry, who'd just gotten married, and Buddy, who's eleven. When I told her about Francie, she said that it was too bad that people had to be born like that. Then I told her how Francie really liked to have people come over because she couldn't get out much, and Tyler said she'd love to come and visit her. She walked home with me the next day and taught Francie how to talk with a Cockney accent. Then she did a little imitation of Mr. Schlitz. Francie thought she was marvelous.

Anyway, when I asked Mr. Schlitz about it, he agreed that attending the creation trial would be a good MGM project. He said he would expect me to give a report to the class when it was over, and then he wrote a note to my counselor suggesting that he sign my release.

The trial started the following Monday. I can't believe it was only two weeks ago. So much has happened since then.

My dad's office is not far from the Superior Court Building where the trial was to be held, so he offered to drop me off there on his way to work. I was wearing my Levi's and a checked blouse and was carrying a copy of *Cosmos* that my dad had given me the night before. He said there was always a lot of waiting around at trials and that that would give me something to read. He said if I was lucky, I might even get Carl Sagan to autograph it. The State of California was planning on calling Dr. Sagan as a witness to testify against the teaching of creation in science classes.

The trial wasn't supposed to start until ten, but my dad said if I wanted to get a seat, I'd better get there early, since there had been a lot of pretrial publicity on TV and in the newspapers, and quite a few people would probably want to be there. One paper had had a headline that read, "Monkey Trial Set for Capital Replay"; the article had told all about how Carl Sagan and twenty-five other scientists, educators, and even ministers were expected to testify for the defense against the teaching of creationism as science. The article said the trial had attracted such wide interest that newspeople were coming in from as far away as Europe to be there.

The newspapers referred to it as a "monkey trial" because they were comparing it to the Scopes trial in Tennessee in 1925, when this teacher named Scopes was tried for teaching evolution in a public school. Scopes was found guilty, even though his lawyer, the famous Clarence Darrow, had made the other lawyer, William Jennings Bryan, look pretty silly. I know so much about the Scopes trial from reading *Inherit the Wind* last year in my English class.

Well, when we got to the courthouse I told Dad goodbye and got out of the car and started walking up the steps toward the door.

That's when I first saw Kurt.

He had just finished locking his bike to a tree out by the front sidewalk and was walking up the steps from the other side. We both got to the big front door at about the same time, so he opened it for me. I smiled and said thanks and he just sort of nodded. He was pretty nice looking, not real tall, probably around 5 feet 9 inches or so, with nice curly brown hair. When we got into the building, he took off his orange backpack and hooked it over his shoulder.

There was no one else around, at least no one that I could see. I walked over to the elevator, since my dad had told me that the trial was going to be on the fourth floor. Kurt was sort of following along, looking all around the building as if he didn't know where to go.

"Excuse me," he said, as I pushed the elevator button, "but do you happen to know where that creation trial is going to be?"

"Yes. That's where I'm going."

"Oh, good."

He followed me into the elevator. Neither of us said anything during the ride up. He stood to one side when the elevator door opened and I got out first. Then we kind of walked down the corridor together.

"Do you know the room number?" he asked.

"Department 14, I think."

We found Department 14 down at the end of the hall. The door to the courtroom was open, so we walked in and looked around.

"Pretty small," Kurt remarked. "Not many seats. Good thing we came early."

"Yeah."

There were only four rows of seats, and the first two rows were blocked off with strips of wide masking tape. We found out later that those rows were reserved for the reporters. There were maybe eight or ten people in the room when we came in, but no one was sitting down. They were all busy, laying some wires along the floor and setting up TV lights and talking to each other. There was one woman — she was wearing jeans and was obviously one of the camera crew. She was crawling along the floor, covering the wires with masking tape. It looked like a fun job. Someone kept turning the bright lamps on and off, and other guys were holding up light meters and things.

"I guess we can just sit down, huh?" Kurt asked softly, looking at me.

"I guess so."

So I sat down in the back row and Kurt sat next to me. He

took a book from his backpack and then shoved the pack under his seat. Then he took off his jacket and draped it over the back of the seat. His gray T-shirt read "University of California — Davis."

"Did you ride your bike here, all the way from Davis?"

"Oh, sure. It's not that far. Twenty miles, maybe."

"That's far."

"Well, I borrowed my brother's racing bike. I wanted to try it out. He paid enough for it."

"Hm."

"He lives in L.A. and he rode all the way from *there* last week."

"Boy. How long did it take him?"

"Well, he and his partner — they're a couple of hot-shot lawyers, you know? — they decided to take a week off and ride eight or nine hundred miles — L.A. to Davis and back again. But when they got here, they were both really shot." He smiled. "Every day they'd say, 'Well, just one more day of rest, and we'll head on back.' Finally I just told them to get in the car and I'd take them to the airport." He laughed. "God, they were relieved as hell." He shook his head and added, "But now I've got to take their bikes back down next weekend. Crazy guys."

Kurt folded his arms and looked around the courtroom. Then he looked at me. "Ever been to a trial before?"

"Nope."

I don't know why, but one of the first things I always notice about boys is their eyes. Kurt's were brown and quick, but softened by long lashes and thick brows. They were what I would call intelligent-looking eyes. I can't explain what intelligent-looking eyes look like, but I know them when I see them.

58

"My name is Kurt. Kurt Rosen." He looked at me, raising those soft, friendly brows.

"Oh!" I said, finally waking up. "I'm Alfie Newton."

"Alfred E. Neuman! *You're* Alfred E. Neuman? Wow. I've always wanted to meet you!"

"Alfie New*ton*," I repeated. Then I added, just to let him know I got the joke, "Now don't make me *mad*."

"Oh no," he groaned, and covered his eyes with his hand. Then he said, "Alfie? Alfie? What kind of a name is that?"

"What do you mean, 'What kind of a name is that?' "

"*Alfie?* Is that a real name?"

You know how, with some people, it seems that you've known them all your life, even though you just met? Well, that's how it was with Kurt. "I was named after my father, dummy. *Alfred.*"

"Your name is *Alfred?*" He looked at me with an incredulous expression, but I knew he was only joking.

Before I could answer he changed the subject. "Hey," he asked, "what's your book? *Cosmos*, huh? Read it yet?"

"Not yet. I just got it last night." I pointed to his book. "What's yours?"

"Oh this? It's just a book on genetics."

"That your major?"

He nodded.

"Gonna be a Genesis, huh?" I'm not my father's daughter for nothing.

Kurt looked up quickly. "No," he said drily, "in the beginning I was, but then I saw the light."

"Hmm. I bet that was a Revelation."

He kind of shook his head and looked disgusted. Pretty soon he said, "No kidding, Alfie, what are you doing here? Shouldn't you be in school?"

"Well, my dad thought I might be interested in what was going to happen here."

"And they let you out of school?"

"Well, I'm doing a special project for my gifted class."

I usually don't tell people I'm in MGM — it's embarrassing. They look at you funny, kind of squinty-eyed. But, somehow, I wanted Kurt to know. He was probably one himself.

By now the courtroom was really filling up fast. There were only a few more empty seats, and the reporters in the first two rows kept sitting down and getting up and sitting down again. They were a restless bunch.

Just then these two TV guys walked up the aisle. One of them had a microphone and the other had a big TV camera perched on his shoulder. All of a sudden this bright light snapped on and they were pointing the camera right at me!

The newsman asked me my name and what school I went to and things like that. Then he said, "How do you feel about this issue? Do you think creation should be taught along with evolution in the science classroom?"

I was really surprised and nervous. I had never been on TV before. I don't know exactly what I said — the exact words, I mean. But I sort of said, sure, I thought that would be fair. I said that I thought the creationists should have a chance to represent their views. "After all," I said, "nobody knows for *sure*, do they?"

The interviewer said thank you and then they shone the light on Kurt. When they asked him what he did, he said he was a graduate student over at Davis. That kind of surprised me, because he didn't look that old. Then the guy asked him if he "agreed with his friend," meaning me, I guess.

Kurt shot me a quick look. "Absolutely not! Creationism is not scientific! It's religious!" He seemed really upset.

"Science is . . . well, it's the arrangement of facts and laws in an orderly system. Religion is . . . ," Kurt hesitated, "Well, I'm sorry, I don't have an exact definition of religion — but it's based on faith. Faith and the supernatural. And faith and the supernatural are definitely *not* science!"

The TV guy said, "Yes, but the creationists claim they *are* scientific."

Kurt nodded. "I know. That's why I'm here. I want to see just how they can attempt to justify that claim."

The guy said thank you and moved on down the row to the next person.

Kurt looked at me in amazement. *"Fair?"* he asked. "My *God,* Alfie!"

6

AFTER KURT LOOKED AT ME LIKE THAT AND said, "My *God,* Alfie!" he slumped down in his seat and shook his head as if I had just made the most stupid remark in history.

I couldn't understand it. "What's wrong with fair, huh?" I asked, nudging him with my arm. "No one knows for sure what happened, do they, Kurt? Were you there? Did you see it all?"

Kurt turned and looked at me with a mixture of impatience and amusement, the way you'd look at a small child who had just colored on the wall.

"Alfie," he started.

But just then things were beginning to happen in the courtroom. There was a lot of hustle and bustle, and the bailiff asked everyone to stand up while the judge came in. Kurt leaned over and whispered in my ear. "We'll talk about it later."

The judge seemed nice. His name was Judge Perluss. There was no jury in this case. I don't know why. Judge Perluss announced that this case was Segraves versus the State of California.

Then he said that the proceedings were going to be televised and he hoped it could be done so as not to interfere with the judicial process. He said that they were setting up a TV monitor in the next room, since this courtroom was obviously too small to accommodate all the people who wanted to watch the proceedings.

Then the creationists' attorney made his statement. His name was Mr. Turner, and he was just an average kind of guy with gray hair and glasses. He seemed pretty smart, though, and he spoke in a nice, natural way, not pompous or anything. He started off by saying that his clients wanted the schools to stop teaching the theory of evolution as a *fact* in public schools.

He went on to say that his clients' First Amendment rights were being abridged. He said his clients' kids were getting confused, and that teaching evolution as fact violated the Constitutional rights of Christian pupils by "offending their religious beliefs." He said the public schools have to accommodate the beliefs of the Christian child.

Kurt moved around uncomfortably in his seat when Mr. Turner said that. He had a pen attached to the neckline of his T-shirt, and he took it out with a little snap and wrote on his book cover for me to see, "What if they believed in little green men? Would we have to accommodate that?"

I just made a face at him.

Mr. Turner was still talking. He said his clients objected to the dogmatism in the Science Framework. I didn't know then what the Science Framework was. I found out later that it was just this booklet that the State Department of Education prints that guides science teachers. It outlines the purposes of science and the important things they should cover in class.

Apparently they have frameworks for most courses of study, such as history and English and math.

Pretty soon they called the first witness. He reminded me of my dad. He worked for the State Department of Education and had something to do with textbooks. He had all these charts up there and had to answer about a million questions about how the state chooses textbooks.

The reporters in the first two rows were taking notes like mad at first, but finally, one by one, they just closed their little notebooks and started yawning. I thought it was interesting though, in a way. I never knew that people went through all that trouble just to pick our textbooks. The books have to pass all kinds of "legal compliances" and content something-or-other and stuff like that. You wouldn't know it, though, if you had to read some of them.

Then the judge said it was time for the lunch recess. Kurt and I decided we'd skip lunch and stay in our seats. There were a lot of people clamoring out in the hallway, and we knew if we left we wouldn't get the seats back again.

But we found out we couldn't do that. The bailiff announced that everyone had to leave. They were closing the courtroom for lunch.

There was a real crush getting out the door. There were a bunch of TV cameras outside and millions of people milling around — a real madhouse. When I finally made it out to the hallway, I looked around and saw that Kurt was still at my side, backpack over his shoulder, hands in his pockets, and clear brown eyes looking steadily into mine.

There was a TV camera blocking our way, so we had to stand there by the door for a little while. We finally got a good look at the kid though — the plaintiff, little Kasey Segraves. We weren't able to see him so well in the courtroom since he was facing toward the front most of the time.

Kasey was just one of the official plaintiffs in the suit. I think the other two were his two brothers, but they weren't there. We got a good look at the father, too — Mr. Kelly Segraves, of the Creation-Science Research Center in San Diego.

Mr. Segraves and Kasey were being interviewed right in front of us. You could tell when someone was being interviewed, because the bright lights would be on.

Kasey Segraves, the little kid, was supposed to be thirteen years old, but looked a lot younger. He looked angelic, he really did, with his blond curly hair and sort of puffed-out rosy cheeks. His father looked something like that too, only older.

After the interview was over, Kurt and I were just standing around, not knowing exactly what to do. We were standing in a little knot of people right by the courtroom door. "I'm pretty hungry," I said, "but if we leave we won't get our seats back."

"We could go next door and watch it on TV."

"Oh yeah, but that's not the same as being there."

"Listen," he said, "there's probably a cafeteria around here somewhere. Why don't you stay here and hold our places, and I'll go get us something to eat?"

"Hey, good idea."

By now the hallway was clearing out pretty fast. After Kurt left, there were only about a dozen of us waiting by the door. I was listening to them talking. This one creationist lady was trying to explain to someone how carbon dating was really inaccurate. They were arguing about the age of the earth. She said it was ten thousand years old, and he said it was over four billion years old. Then this other guy with real short gray hair spoke up. "Excuse me," he said politely to the creationist lady, "but you don't know what you're talking about." So then the two of them started arguing.

I can't remember what they said, but everyone else was just standing around listening to them. They were arguing pretty good-naturedly though, and at one point even introduced themselves to each other. She was Adele, and he was Ralph. Even though he had gray hair, he wasn't that old.

Pretty soon Kurt came back with a couple of sandwiches, a cup of coffee, and a carton of milk. "I didn't know if you drank coffee or milk," he said, "so I got one of each. Which would you like?"

"Oh, the milk, I guess. If that's all right. I don't drink coffee much."

"Fine."

I asked him how much I owed him and he told me, so I just gave him the money. I thought that was really classy of him. Gregg, for instance, would insist on paying for mine, and I'd have to argue, and he would refuse to take it, and we'd end up wasting a lot of time and everybody would feel terrible.

"So what's been going on here?" he asked.

I turned and faced the wall and leaned my head sideways, my hand to my mouth. "They're arguing about carbon dating," I whispered.

"Oh, Jesus. Wouldn't you know it."

Then that guy Ralph started talking to Kurt. "Excuse me," he said, "but I overheard you talking to the young lady here this morning. You're a grad student at UC Davis?"

Kurt nodded. "Yes."

"Do you happen to know G. Ledyard Stebbins over there?"

"Oh, sure."

"I hear he has a new book coming out soon."

"On evolution. Yes, I know." Then Kurt asked him, "What do you do?"

"I'm with the U.S. Geological Survey."

Kurt nodded.

"Actually," Ralph added, "I'm here in California on vacation for a few days, visiting my wife's family. When I heard about this trial, I couldn't believe it! I had to see it for myself."

"It is hard to believe," Kurt agreed.

Ralph looked around and then leaned closer to me and Kurt. "Some fellow out in the corridor just told me in all seriousness that *Noah's flood* is responsible for the earth's geological sediments and the fossil record!" He shook his head. "To hear something like that in this day and age, really. . . ."

Just then someone in the crowd shouted, "Hey, they're opening the door!" You wouldn't believe all the pushing and shoving that started. The people sitting over on the benches all flocked over and crowded in. It was really a mess.

Kurt grabbed my arm and we got carried along in the flow, but not far enough. The bailiff was counting people off as they entered the courtroom, and when he got to twenty-four he said, "Sorry, folks. That's it. You'll have to go next door. There's a TV monitor next door."

"That's not fair!" I wailed. "I was waiting here the whole time!"

Ralph laughed. "Did you see those creationists? Pretty pushy for Christians, wouldn't you say?"

Adele, the lady he was arguing with earlier, folded her arms and looked him right in the eye. "Some of those people were evolutionists, Ralph!"

Ralph grinned. "Survival of the fittest, Adele."

"Come on," Kurt said. "It doesn't make any difference. Let's just go next door and watch it on the monitor."

The afternoon session was just about the same as the morning one — on and on about how textbooks are selected. You wouldn't believe it. I was wishing they'd just get on with the arguments about creation versus evolution. That's what I had come to hear.

Being in the room with the TV monitor was a lot different from being in the real courtroom. People were whispering to each other and reading newspapers, and one lady was even knitting. Kurt and I didn't talk, though. I could tell he wanted to listen to what was being said, even though nothing of interest happened all afternoon. Finally, I guess the judge had enough. He called a recess until ten o'clock the next morning.

Kurt stretched out his legs for a minute, and then we both stood up. Out in the corridor there was the same madhouse scene as at noon. The reporters were grabbing the lawyers and the Segraves family and even some of the spectators. I felt like a celebrity.

Kurt and I threaded our way through the crowd to the elevators. "It's been really nice talking with you all day, Alfie," he said, as we stepped into the elevator. "Coming back tomorrow?"

"Oh, sure. Are you?"

"I don't know. I'll have to see how it goes."

Our elevator arrived at the main floor, and I made my way to the front doors of the building. Kurt was right behind me.

"Well, how you getting home?" he asked, when we were out on the sidewalk. It was like we didn't want to say goodbye.

"I'm walking, part way, anyway. Then I'll probably take the bus. But first I've got to stop and pick up a poster I had made for a friend. It's supposed to be ready this afternoon."

Kurt raised those eyebrows again, teasing. "A *friend*?"

"Yeah. It's *her* birthday tomorrow."

We were over by the tree now, where his bike was parked.

"Well, where is it? I'll walk over there with you."

"The poster place?" I pointed down the street. "It's just a block up that way, then over."

He knelt to unlock the bike. "So, this poster you're going to pick up, is for your *girl*friend, eh?"

"That's right. Her name is Tyler."

"Hmm. And how's the old *boy*friend situation? That's what I'd like to know!"

"Are you kidding?" I laughed nervously. Then I added, "Well, there's this one guy that keeps hanging around. His name's Gregg." I didn't want Kurt to think that *no* one was interested in me.

"Only one guy? Come on. Old Kurt knows better than that!"

It was kind of fun, talking to him like that. With Kurt, you just felt like telling him everything. So I said, "But then there's this other guy at school, Victor Beauchamp."

"Old Victor, huh?"

"He's really smart."

"Yeah?"

"And he has these nice green eyes."

"But he doesn't pay any attention to you," Kurt broke in.

"That's right! How did you know?"

"Ah, I know *exactly* how he feels." Kurt looked up toward the sky, pretending he was trying hard to remember. "Oh, my high school days — so long ago."

"Come on!"

"Listen, Alfie," he said, coming back to earth, "he's probably just shy. Scared to death. Seriously. That's how I was."

I looked at him in exaggerated amazement.

He laughed. "No kidding."

We were almost to the poster shop by then. Kurt playfully pushed the bike sideways in front of me, blocking my path.

I looked at him. The late afternoon sun was shining on his curls and his brown eyes were full of golden speckles. "You're a brainy and good-looking kid, Alfie," he said, "and if this Victor Beauchamp character can't see that, well. . . ."

This nice little chill just went right through me when he said that, all the way down and all the way up again.

Kurt wheeled his bike right into the shop, and we waited while the guy went to the back room to get the poster. It was slightly embarrassing waiting there, since they had a lot of posters in there of girls, sort of nude types. Actually, it was a pretty sleazy place. But Kurt was real cool. He just glanced around once, and then he ignored them and started talking to me.

"What's this poster of, anyway?"

"Oh, wait and see. I want to see if you know who it is."

Just then the guy came in from the back and unrolled it. It was a picture of Garry Trudeau I had found in an old *Time* magazine that was out in the shed. I had found it about two months ago, but I didn't show it to Tyler. She really loves Doonesbury. In the picture, old Garry is real young, and he's standing there in a T-shirt with his thumbs in his jeans. God, it's so cute. Tyler's going to go crazy when she realizes who it is. I'm giving her the article, too. I know she'll like it.

"Hey!" Kurt exclaimed. "Garry Trudeau! Where did you get the picture?"

"You knew who it was!"

"Sure. Where did you get it?"

"Out of an old *Time* magazine."

"Oh, sure! I remember it now. It was a cover story, four or five years ago."

"Boy, you must be really old to remember that."

"Yep."

70

"No kidding, Kurt. How old are you?"

He hesitated, but only for a second. "I'm twenty-three."

"You don't look that old."

"Clean living."

"I'll bet."

We left the store and just stood there on the sidewalk.

"Well," Kurt said, adjusting his backpack, "where do you catch the bus?"

I pointed to the corner. "Right there."

"Well then, I guess I'll be shoving off."

I was racking my brain like crazy, trying to think of something to say, something that would keep him there for a few minutes longer. But my mind was a complete blank.

He slipped his foot into the pedal clip.

Think of something, you dummy! I told myself.

But he had already pushed off. He raised his hand in a little farewell wave and said casually, "See you around, Alfie."

The minute he was gone I thought of something I could have said. I could have said, "Hey, what do you have against *fairness*, anyway? What's wrong with being *fair* in the science classroom?" But I had missed my chance. He was gone now, and I might never see him again.

I looked up the street and there wasn't a bus in sight, so I started to walk.

"See you around," he had said. But everybody says that all the time. It didn't mean anything.

Or did it?

I kept walking along, gazing at the trash in the gutter and the weeds along the side of the road. It was a beautiful sight, in a way. Torn candy wrappers and old beer cans and spindly weeds can actually be beautiful, if you look at them in an unprejudiced way. *See you around.* Suddenly, for no apparent reason, my heart soared. He'd be at the trial the next day. He had to be.

It was almost dark by the time I got home. Aunt Marion and Francie were watching TV. The news had just started. Francie was in her wheelchair, and her head drooped over to one side. She looked really tired. Apparently she had already eaten. Her half-empty dish was sitting on the coffee table.

"What's happening?" I asked.

"Your father's out jogging and your mom's getting groceries." Aunt Marion was stretched out on the couch.

I went over and kissed Francie on the forehead. "Hi, honey. You didn't eat much. What's wrong?"

She pulled down her lower lip with her fingers. "My canker sore," she said, talking funny. "It hurts when I eat." She let her lip go. "Dr. Amos came over today."

"Oh?"

"He says I'm okay."

I shot a glance over to Aunt Marion, but she didn't bat an eye.

"And Ma Johnson came over too!" Francie said. "See the spoon she brought me?"

Ma Johnson was this really nice lady that worked in the children's room at our church. Her real name was Alma, but all the kids called her Ma. She told my parents once that, if anything ever happened to them, she would be happy to take Francie. My mom thought that was about the kindest, most loving gesture anyone could make.

I took up the spoon from the table. "How cute," I said. "A Mickey Mouse spoon."

Francie smiled. "Ma Johnson said Mickey will help me eat more."

I nodded. "It's nice," I said.

I looked up at the TV. Tyler's father was on the news. Did I mention that he's a TV anchorman? He does the local stuff. He's a pretty nice guy in person. He likes to talk a lot, but he's not boring, and he listens when you're talking. Lots of times people who talk a lot never listen.

All of a sudden, on TV, he said something about the creation trial attracting nationwide attention. And there *I* was, on the screen! Really! For about one-tenth of a second. Kurt, too. "Look!" I shouted. "That's me!"

Old Francie got really excited, too. "I saw you! I did!"

Aunt Marion just laughed. "The phone will start ringing any minute. Hollywood calling."

"Oh, that reminds me," I said. "I've got to call Tyler. Tomorrow's her birthday, and I don't know how I can get to see her. I don't know *if* I can get to see her. I have a nice present for her, too." I unrolled the poster. "See?" Of course they didn't know who it was.

When the commercial came on, I started to walk over to the phone. Just as I got there, it rang. It was Tyler.

"Hey!" I said. "I was just going to call you!"

"Must be ESP," she said, joking.

She was calling to invite me out to dinner the following night to celebrate her birthday.

"My parents are taking me and Buddy and some other people out for dinner in a swanky restaurant, and they said I could invite you along," she said.

"Hey, that's great!"

"And there'll be a little surprise for you!"

"For me?" I asked. "What?"

"Oh," she said, "you'll see."

Tyler loves to play games like that. I usually don't pay too much attention. "Oh, come on," I said. "Don't be so mysterious."

"Okay, I'll give you a hint. I won't be the only person in the restaurant having a birthday. And that's all I'm going to say."

Then she got businesslike. "They want to go around seven, or as soon as my dad can get away from the station. Where can we pick you up? Will you be home, or what?"

"Gee. I don't know. I don't know what time they'll finish tomorrow. You know, at the courthouse."

"Maybe we could pick you up downtown someplace," she suggested. "How about the library? It's near the courthouse."

"Sure," I agreed. "I'll just wait for you at the library."

"Right."

"And I'll call you back tonight if it's not okay. But it should be all right."

"Okay. And Alfie, guess what? I saw you on TV just now."

"No you didn't. I was only on for half a second."

"Well, I saw you. You were wearing your checked blouse. Right?"

"I'll be darned. Old eagle-eyes."

"Who was that cute guy sitting next to you?"

"*What?*"

She laughed. "Never mind. You can tell me about him tomorrow."

"Tyler, I'm speechless."

"Well, no sense keeping you on the phone then. See you tomorrow — the library, around seven."

"Okay Tyler. So long."

After she hung up, I started thinking about what she had

said about a surprise for me. She wouldn't be the only one in the restaurant having a birthday. And then it hit me. I got a sudden attack of gooseflesh as I realized that on the following night I would be having dinner in a swanky restaurant seated next to the one and only Victor Beauchamp!

Pretty soon my dad got home and took a shower, and then my mom got home and started fixing dinner. While she was doing that, Aunt Marion and I got Francie to bed. She had these huge dark circles under her eyes, and her skin was almost transparent. She was trembling as I touched her hand and told her goodnight.

"Come here, Alfie," she whispered.

I bent down, close to her face, and pushed her thin hair away from her forehead. "What, honey?"

"I don't believe Dr. Amos," she said in her breathy whisper. The look in her eyes reminded me of the wounded fawn in the food chain program. I couldn't stand it.

"Don't worry, honey." I couldn't believe I could make my voice sound so confident. What a terrific liar I'd make. "Everything will be okay," I said. "You go to sleep now. I'll tell Mom and Dad you're ready to say goodnight."

Her eyes searched mine. Her lids were heavy. "Okay," she said finally. "Goodnight, Alfie."

We had Original Joe hamburger patties and homemade french fries for dinner. My mom makes really good french fries. Someone forgot to bring the ketchup to the table, and as I was walking back from the kitchen with it, Aunt Marion remarked that she never noticed it before, but, boy, I sure did have wide feet. She's always telling me things like that. One time she told me my earlobes were abnormal. She's really full of compliments.

I asked if it would be okay if Tyler and her parents picked me up at the library the next night and took me out with them for her birthday dinner. It was. Nobody else had much to say. I didn't ask what Dr. Amos had said, but I knew it wasn't good by the way they all avoided the subject. My stomach started to hurt.

After dinner, I helped put the dishes in the dishwasher, then I went up to my room and read three chapters of *Cosmos*.

I didn't think about Francie until after I switched off my bedside lamp. And then, before I knew what was happening, I was praying for her again. *Please, please, Jesus — God. Don't let her suffer. Don't let her be afraid.* I got myself into that old familiar trance. I started making bargains. *I'll stop doubting.* I felt like I was in another sphere, another zone — a space-warp, a time-warp. I *knew* God was listening. Pretty soon the feeling went away. I turned the light on again, just for a second, and saw that everything was still the same. Then I turned it off again. I put my face to the pillow and started to cry.

7

I HAVE THIS OLD SHOEBOX UNDER MY BED where I save articles that I clip out of the newspaper. I have some pretty interesting articles in there. For example, there's one that says that kids who get high grades in school have more zinc in their hair than kids who get lower grades. I'm not kidding. And this isn't an article from the *National Enquirer,* either. It was a report in our regular paper about a meeting of the American Chemical Society. I quoted that article to my mom when we were talking one time about how much people could really help how they are. I'm beginning to think that a lot of it depends on things like your brain chemicals and hormones. I mean, if we could really help how we are, we'd all be perfect, wouldn't we? Isn't it a lot more fun being perfect than being some poor drunk in the gutter, or in jail or someplace? Of course, my mom doesn't agree with that at all. So I showed her the zinc article and then I said, "Okay, suppose a kid has a low zinc level in his hair and gets bad grades. Is it still his fault?" She said she couldn't see what that had to do with it.

"But Mom," I said. "Don't you see?" And I explained the whole thing to her again.

"Alfie," she said finally, "you are a very strange child."

While I was getting dressed on Tuesday morning, I was thinking about a long article I have about high-heeled shoes. Some orthopedist was quoted as saying that high heels really wreck women's bodies by throwing everything out of kilter. And then some feminist or other said that women keep harping about equality, and then they voluntarily wear three-inch heels and pantyhose. A psychologist explained it all, though. He said most men enjoy seeing women in high heels. For some unknown reason, men think high-heeled shoes are sexy. Sometimes I think I'm living in an enormous insane asylum.

I was wearing high heels on Tuesday because of Tyler's dinner that night. As I sat there on the edge of my bed, fastening the straps on my shoes, I felt like I was giving in to the illogical environment that surrounded me. Not that Tyler or her parents would care what I wore. They're not snobby like that or anything. But I knew Tyler was going to dress up, and I somehow felt compelled to do the same. That's one big difference right there between Tyler and me. She loves to dress up. But that's only the actress in her coming out. When she dresses up, it's like she's pretending, so that's okay.

But I have a real problem with clothes. It's almost like I don't *want* to look good. It's really hard to explain, but I think lots of times the main reason people want to dress up in all their nice clothes is to make other people feel bad, even though they wouldn't admit it in a million years. They probably haven't even thought about it, really. Nobody ever really *thinks* about anything. But when you do stop and think about it, isn't it a pretty selfish thing to do, spending all that time and money just trying to make people envious?

And it does take a lot of time. My mom and I spent four

hours going around to yardage stores trying to find some blouse material and ribbon to match the ultra-suede suit she made for me. Four hours! And we weren't the only ones. The yardage stores were full of women doing the same thing. And their little kids were all crying in their strollers and dropping their pacifiers all over the floor. God, it was depressing. People's priorities are all mixed up. I don't see why everyone doesn't just wear jogging suits or Levi's all the time.

I looked at myself in the full-length mirror in the hallway that morning, and I must admit I thought I looked pretty good in my ultra-suede suit. I wondered if Kurt would be at the trial that day. If he was, would he look at me any differently? I had the feeling he thought of me as a little sister or something, maybe when he saw me dressed up. . . . And what about Victor?

Suddenly I had to smile. There was old Alfie Newton, who up till now had never really thought that much about boys, all of a sudden thinking about *two* of them.

I brushed some loose threads off my skirt and decided I was going to have to try to get over my warped feelings about clothes someday. Maybe that's one reason why my mom didn't — I almost said didn't love me, but I knew that wasn't true. I knew she loved me, it's just that we were so different.

Francie now, well, she was a lot like my mom. Take the clothes thing, for instance. I keep remembering the time the three of us were out looking at silk scarves to go with one of my mom's dresses. It was just before Francie got worse this last time. Anyway, I was anxious to get finished shopping, so I just pulled the first scarf I could reach off the rack and said, "How about this one?"

Francie looked at me like I just came down from Mars. "Alfie!" she exclaimed. "Mom's dress is a flowered print!"

I looked at the red, white, and blue scarf in my hand and

immediately realized what she meant. But I was in one of those antagonistic moods that shopping always seems to put me in, so I waved the scarf in front of Francie's nose and said in my most sarcastic tone, "So?"

Francie looked at Mom with a face that said more than a thousand words, but she only vocalized four. "Boy, Mom, she's hopeless!"

That made me really mad. "What did you say, you little pip-squeak?"

Now Mom was beginning to get upset with me. "Alfie," she said, "why don't you go over and save us a table at the coffee shop? Francie and I will finish up here and meet you there in a few minutes.

"Trying to get rid of me, huh?" I said, but I was only half joking.

"No. Of course not. It's not that at all." Poor Mom. I know she felt like she was right in the middle.

"Oh, *okay!*" I said grudgingly. "I'll see you at Mel's. But I sure hope you don't take all day!"

They both breathed little sighs of relief, and as I walked away, I could see them out of the corner of my eye, comparing scarves and murmuring in complete agreement with each other.

"This one's too dull."

"Hm. Yes, I think so too."

By the time I reached the coffee shop I had cooled down a little, and the whole incident had even started to seem funny. I had to smile, remembering Francie's shocked expression. She was a prim little thing and sure didn't have much of a sense of humor. I'll bet my mom was just like her when she was a kid. I guess they couldn't help it, though. It was in their chemicals.

I ordered a Coke and watched the people on the mall for a

while. Then I started in on one of my more recent day-
dreams. It was suggested to me by Mr. Burr, actually, although he was only joking when he said it. It happened during
the first week of calculus. Mr. Burr was giving us a little in-
troduction to the subject, and he said that calculus was invented around the year 1666 by Sir Isaac Newton, perhaps
the greatest scientific genius who ever lived. He paused a
minute, looked at me and said, "One of your ancestors, perhaps?"

And then old Jeremy Hobson, who's really nice but is
flunking calculus, called out, "So *that* explains it!"

Anyway, that's what I was daydreaming about — that
maybe I was a descendant of Isaac Newton. I got a magical
feeling all over just thinking that maybe Isaac Newton's genes
were in my body.

I was still thinking about it when I saw Mom coming up
the center of the mall pushing Francie's wheelchair at an un-
usually fast clip. They came over to where I was waiting, and
Mom got Francie all settled and then she sat down beside me.

"Well," she said cheerily, "I see you got us the best table."

"Huh?"

"This is our favorite table, isn't it, Francie?" she asked,
prompting.

"Oh, yes! It really is."

I could see immediately what they were trying to do, especially after Mom dug around in her shopping bag a minute
and pulled out that stupid red, white, and blue scarf. "This
really *is* a beautiful scarf, Alfie. We decided it would go perfectly with my blue. . . ."

Old Francie was nodding like mad. It was really funny.

"Listen, you two," I broke in. "You didn't hurt my feelings any. I don't care *beans* about scarves, for gods' sake!"

Mom winced slightly at my expletive, but for once she didn't say anything about it. Instead, she said, "It *would* be nice, though, if you would take a little more interest in clothes, darling."

I could feel a backhanded compliment coming on. "You have a very nice little figure, if only you'd. . . ."

"Mom, *please!*"

She looked over at Francie and shrugged helplessly, the two of them aligned again. But I really didn't care. I really didn't.

"Hey, Mom," I said after a short silence, "do you happen to know anything about Dad's family tree?"

She seemed relieved that I wanted to change the subject. "No, darling," she said brightly, picking up the menu, "only that his grandfather was born in Wisconsin."

She didn't ask me why I wanted to know.

That evening, the old clothes argument resurfaced. Mom was upset because she found out I was planning to wear my Levi's on an MGM trip to an afternoon symphony performance.

"You simply can't wear those jeans everywhere," she began, and we were off and running for the umpteenth time. Dad was in the room, too, reading the paper. I told Mom I thought that devoting all that time to how you looked was stupid and egotistical and that it made me uncomfortable. And my mom answered that there was nothing wrong with taking a little pride in how you looked. Well, I jumped right on her then, and said I thought pride was one of the seven deadly sins. And then, to gild the lily, I quoted Matthew. "And why take you thought for raiment, so much, Mom?" I asked. "Consider the lilies of the field."

It wasn't too nice of me, actually. And Dad made it even worse. He lowered his paper and said sarcastically, "Will the *real* Christian please stand up?"

Things got pretty tense then. My mom turned red and started blinking her eyes real fast, but she didn't say anything. I felt sorry for her right away, and I wanted to apologize, but I didn't. It's really hard to apologize sometimes, even though you know you should. I still feel bad about that.

Anyway, on Tuesday, the second day of the trial, since I was going out to dinner at a swanky restaurant, I just bit the bullet and put on my one good outfit — that ultra-suede suit my mom made for me and my four-hour blouse and my one pair of heels, which I hate.

I was still combing my hair when Dad started up the motor. So I ran around gathering up Tyler's poster, which I had rolled up and tied with a big yellow ribbon, and my mom's purse which she loves to let me borrow, and stumbled out to the car.

Of course the first thing I looked for as we drove up to the courthouse was Kurt's bike parked by the tree. It wasn't there.

I said goodbye to Dad and walked up the steps. When I got to the door, I remember I had this funny feeling, like I had forgotten something, or that something was wrong. And then I realized that I was still thinking about Kurt's not being there.

I was early enough to get a seat in the courtroom, so I just sat down and read until the bailiff came in and announced, "Will everyone please stand."

We all stood up while Judge Perluss entered the courtroom from a door behind the bench. It was really quiet in there. No one was whispering or anything.

Both the Segraves, the father and the son, were called to testify that day. They both said about the same thing. They both said, "I believe that God created man, as man, and put him on the earth." They must have said that about fifteen times.

Mr. Segraves testified that the creation of man by God is a

central, fundamental, and basic necessity in their religious belief.

Then the judge asked the kid more about what his teacher had said about evolution. The kid said that his teacher told him that man evolved from the apes. Then the kid said that his father told him that God created man, as man, and put him on earth. The kid said he was confused. He said that he believed his father, but that the teacher was confusing him. I felt sorry for him. He seemed like a nice kid. He reminded me of Francie.

Then we recessed for lunch and the bailiff herded us all out of the courtroom. I got right into the line by the door to wait for the afternoon session. I had decided earlier that I would just skip lunch that day. I was going to have a big dinner anyway.

There were eight or ten people ahead of me in the line. That guy Ralph was way up there in the front. The corridor was a madhouse again — millions of reporters and TV cameras and all that. And I was still looking for Kurt, too. But I didn't see him around there anyplace.

The case really took a different twist that afternoon. All of a sudden, it seems, the creationists changed their whole case. It surprised the judge and everybody else too.

The whole thing hinged on the Science Framework. Under questioning, Mr. Segraves said that he would be willing to settle the whole issue if the State would just *amend* the Science Framework. He said all he wanted now was some indication in there that the evolutionary theory is not universally accepted as true. He said all he wanted was that evolution be presented as a "belief of some scientists, not as a fact."

Boy, when he said that, a murmur went all through the courtroom. Some of the reporters looked at each other and raised their eyebrows in surprise. Mr. Robert Tyler, the

84

defense attorney, looked like he had just been hit with a baseball bat. And the judge said in a high-pitched, surprised voice, "But I thought you wanted scientific creationism *taught* in the schools!"

One of the reporters in the row ahead of me snapped shut his notebook and whispered to the buy next to him, "Well, that's it! There goes the State's whole case."

"What do you mean?" the other guy asked.

"It's simple. Since the creationists are no longer demanding equal time in the classroom, there'll be no need to hear all the scientists the State had lined up. This case is over."

The judge continued to look amazed. He said that what he had visualized as a "great and constitutional case has evolved — excuse me — has come down to semantics!"

Some people smiled when he changed the word "evolved" to "come down to," but he just shook his head and added, "Well, it seems to me it's a long road to a little house."

I looked over and spotted Ralph right across the aisle. He smiled at me. I think you could call it a rueful smile. Then he cupped his hands around his face and mouthed some words I couldn't make out. I guess he noticed my puzzled look, because he mouthed them again. This time I understood him. He said, "They chickened out."

After Judge Perluss recessed the court until the next day, I walked over to the library. To tell the truth, I was starting to get a little nervous over the prospect of having dinner with old Green-eyes. The only thought that saved me was the realization that there were going to be lots of other people there.

I sat down at a table in the library and worried about Victor for a few minutes more. I sure hoped I wasn't going to say or do anything stupid that night. Then I realized that worrying about it wasn't getting me anywhere.

I went over to the religious section and got down a Bible.

85

I wanted to read Genesis again. The Segraves had said over and over in court that day that they believed *God created man, as man, and put him on earth.*

I opened the Bible and read those beautiful words again — how God had created Adam out of the clay, and how God put Adam to sleep and removed a rib, from which He made Eve. Then the serpent tempted Eve and she disobeyed God. And so did Adam.

I put the Bible aside and thought about Adam and Eve disobeying God. That was the all-important Original Sin, the backbone of the Christian faith, and the real reason for Jesus. I suddenly realized that was exactly what Mr. Segraves was trying to say during his testimony. He said the Genesis story was central, fundamental, and basic to their religious belief. I understood now what he had meant about all of us being sinners.

I folded my arms on the table and rested my head on them and thought about Mr. Segraves and the creationists, and about my mom, and even about what Mr. Burr had said about his church. Boy, religion was sure complicated.

I guess I fell asleep, because the next thing I knew, someone was tapping me on the shoulder.

"Hey!" Tyler said. "Wake up! Let's go!"

I picked up my purse and the poster from the table and went and put the Bible back.

As soon as we were out the door, I blurted out, "So where's Victor, you rat!"

Tyler laughed. "You figured it out, huh? They're meeting us at the restaurant. This is going to be so much fun! I can hardly wait to see you two together!"

"Tyler, will you stop that! Come on, now. Quit it!"

Her parents and her little brother were waiting for us in the car. The restaurant was just a few blocks away. Mr. Harmon dropped us off in front and went around the back to park the car.

Tyler wasn't kidding when she called it a swanky restaurant. The waiters were all wearing tuxedos, and you could hear the muted clinking of glasses and quiet conversations punctuated by soft laughter. We waited in the little foyer for Mr. Harmon. When he came in, he went right to the hostess and said, "We have a reservation. Harmon, party of eight."

"Oh, yes. Right this way," she said. "The rest of your party is already seated."

Tyler reached over and gave me a pinch. "Already seated," she mugged.

She was making me so nervous I could hardly walk straight. The men, Mr. Beauchamp and Victor that is, stood up as we approached the table. Tyler introduced me to Victor's parents, and then there was that usual confusion when people are trying to get seated. By the way Tyler was scampering around there, it was obvious to me that she had planned for Victor and me to sit next to each other, but somehow things got shuffled around, and I ended up between Tyler and her little brother. Victor was across the table, seated between his mother and father.

Tyler made a motion to draw her chair closer to the table, at the same time leaning close to my ear. "Curses!" she whispered. "Foiled again!"

As soon as we were all settled, the cocktail waitress appeared and asked if anyone would like a drink. The grown-ups decided they'd skip the cocktails and just have wine with their dinner.

During the pause after the cocktail waitress left, Mrs. Harmon made some comment about how nice I looked. "I think this is the first time I've ever seen you in a dress," she said. She didn't say it critically though. She's not like that. "It looks very nice," she added.

"Thank you," I said. "It's a suit." I immediately wanted to bite my tongue off. I shouldn't have corrected her like that, but she didn't seem to notice.

"These girls just *live* in their jeans," she said, indicating Tyler and me.

"Oh yes, these kids nowadays!" Mr. Harmon added in mock irritation, and we all laughed in a reserved, obligatory fashion.

For the first time that night I had a chance to really look at Victor. He looked like he'd been up all night reading *War and Peace* or *The Brothers Karamazov* or something. I really liked that serious, meditative look, but I was beginning to wonder if he *ever* smiled.

"Are you enjoying the trial, Alfie?" Mr. Beauchamp asked as we all started to look at our menus.

I was taken by surprise for a minute, and before I could answer he explained that he had seen me there. Mr. Beauchamp was a newspaper reporter and was assigned to the trial.

"You know," he remarked, "it's a funny thing about that trial. I was chatting with a reporter for the *Manchester Guardian* this morning. He said his paper told him to write something short and funny. He said to me, 'My God, you Americans have sent a man to the moon, and you're still arguing about Adam and Eve!' "

"That's interesting," I said, feeling like I was playing the part of a young lady in some "Masterpiece Theatre" production.

There was some general light discussion then about what looked good on the menu, and pretty soon this very professional-looking waiter walked up and asked if we were ready to order. Mr. Harmon looked around and most of us nodded, and he said yes.

The waiter started off with Tyler. He was standing by her right shoulder with his little notebook and a very attentive look. "Are you ready, miss?" he asked.

"Yes. I would like the New York Steak dinner, please."

"The six-ounce steak, or the ten-ounce?"

"Ten-ounce, please."

"And how would you like that cooked?"

"Ah . . . medium rare, please."

"Would you like soup or salad with your dinner?"

"What kind of soup do you have?"

"The soups this evening are cream of broccoli and French onion."

"I would like the salad, please."

"What kind of dressing would you like on your salad?"

"Uh . . ."

"We have Roquefort, Italian, Thousand Island. . . ."

"Thousand Island would be fine."

"Would you like french fries or baked potato?"

"Baked, please."

"Sour cream with chives or butter?"

"Yes, please."

"Which?"

"Pardon?"

"Would you like sour cream with chives or butter?"

"Could I have both?"

"Certainly, miss. And would you like corn bread or a dinner roll?"

Tyler sighed. "Dinner roll, please."

"And what would you like to drink?"

"A Coke, please."

"Large or small?"

"Large, please."

"Fine. Thank you." The waiter started to turn to me, but then he remembered something and looked at Tyler again. "Excuse me," he said, "but would you like your Coke now, or with your dinner?"

"Now, please."

The waiter nodded seriously. "Very good." Then he touched his middle finger to his tongue and quickly flipped the page of his little order book.

I really couldn't see the sense of going through that routine again. The waiter took a step toward me, and, pencil poised, he asked solicitously, "Now, what would you like?"

"The same," I said.

Everyone at the table looked up. The waiter seemed taken aback. "The same?" he repeated blankly.

Across the table, Victor was the first to laugh. It started off as a low giggle, but in a second it was a full-blown laughing fit.

I loved it. I think what I loved most about it was that it was a one hundred percent genuine laughing fit. Victor didn't go in for any fake laughs.

Everyone seemed to relax after that. Even the waiter shook his head and smiled and turned into a real person.

I didn't say much during dinner. The conversation was mostly like that of old friends — lots of laughter and reminiscing about past birthday parties and summer weekends at the lake and funny little jokes they had played on one another in years gone by. For the first time in my life, I felt a real sense of regret about my own family. I couldn't believe families could be so happy.

I was the only one who had brought a present. After

dessert, Tyler pointed to the poster and asked slyly, "What's that? Is it for me?"

I handed it to her and she unrolled it with a flourish.

She knew it was *somebody*, but she just couldn't pin him down.

"Let's see it," Victor said, and Tyler turned it so he could see. He didn't know who it was either. A vision of Kurt flashed through my mind. But then, Kurt knew everything.

"Who *is* that?" Tyler was saying softly to herself. "I *know* who that is . . ." and then she exclaimed, "God! Is that *Garry Trudeau?* Oh, it is! Oh, he's so cute! Where did you *find* that, Alfie? Oh, I *love* it!"

Later, we said goodbye to the Beauchamps in the restaurant parking lot. Victor was polite enough, but I noticed he didn't grab me passionately and say he couldn't possibly live another day without me.

It was after ten by the time I got home. Francie was in bed, of course, and so was Aunt Marion. Dad was watching TV, as usual, and Mom was reading.

I went straight to the kitchen to get a Coke, and my mom came after me. I took one look at her and knew right away that something had happened. There was a kind of inward glow about her, almost as if someone had just told her a wonderful secret.

We sat down at the table and she asked me if I had a nice time and all that. I just nodded. She had taken something out of the pocket of her robe, and while we were sitting there, she just kept holding it in her hands as if it were some kind of sacred object. I finally saw what it was. It was that Mickey Mouse spoon that old Ma Johnson had given to Francie.

That's when Mom suddenly leaned forward and gently placed the spoon on the table between us.

"Alma Johnson died this morning, Alfie. She just had a stroke and died."

"Oh!" I said. "That's awful!"

That's when my mom said something that really knocked me for a loop. She reached over and put both her hands on my arm. "Alfie," she said, her eyes intent on mine, "I think the Lord has called Alma Johnson for a very special reason." She paused and clasped my arm. "I'm sure the Lord has called Alma so that she can be there to welcome our Francie."

I suddenly felt like I was going to faint. I was stunned by what she was suggesting. "Oh, Mom," I whispered, "don't. . . ."

"Alfie," my mom said, tears clouding her eyes, "our Lord is so good."

Just then my dad walked into the kitchen, and my mom kind of jumped when she saw him. He went over to the coffee maker and poured out the last cup.

"Hi, Alfie," he said.

Mom stood up then and cleared her throat. It was like she was a different person.

My dad was stooped over now, rummaging around in the refrigerator. My mother started rinsing out the empty coffee carafe. My dad found an apple, took a big bite, and headed back to the TV with his coffee cup in one hand and the apple in the other.

"Well, I guess I'll be going to bed," Mom said, drying her hands. She paused in the doorway. "Francie had a very bad day today," she said quietly. "Dr. Amos said he can't understand how her heart just keeps beating."

When she said that, I got a sick feeling in my chest. It started in my chest, sort of, and then went down into my stomach. I don't think I said anything.

"She'd like to talk to you," Mom said. "She said she'd like to talk to you."

"Oh, gees! And I've been gone all day!"

"Well, maybe you can see her in the morning, before you and your father leave, if she's awake." She turned to go. "What would you like for breakfast?"

My mom is big on breakfasts. She insists on cooking eggs and bacon and pancakes and all that kind of stuff. Lots of times my father would just eat some toast and a bite or two of the rest of it. My mom would take the plate away with a sigh, but the next morning there she'd be, cooking all that stuff again. The way I figured it, her mental picture of a good housewife included fixing picture-book breakfasts, whether people wanted them or not.

When she asked me what I wanted for breakfast, I just said, "Oh, Mom, nothing, really. You don't have to fix breakfast. Why don't you just stay in bed? I can make some toast and coffee for Dad."

"Don't be silly," she answered. "Well, I'll think of something."

As it turned out, I didn't have to wait for morning to talk to Francie. I heard some commotion about three in the morning and realized it was Aunt Marion in there, tending to her, turning her over. Aunt Marion had night duty that week. I got up and went in. Francie was wide awake. Aunt Marion was changing the sheet. Francie had really been perspiring a lot lately.

"Ahhh!" Aunt Marion said. "You scared me! What are you doing up, anyway? Or did you just get in?" She knew I hadn't just gotten in. That was just the way she talked.

"Hi, Aunt Marion. I'll finish up. You can go back to bed."

"Swell," she said. She kissed Francie lightly on the forehead. "Goodnight, baby. Sleep well."

"Could you turn off the light, please?" Francie asked me. "It's so bright." It was only about a fifteen-watt bulb in there, but her eyes were really sensitive, I guess.

I turned off the light and I could hardly see her. She has — she had this little angel night-light though, and pretty soon I could see okay by that.

"How are you doing?" I asked softly.

"I'm doing fine. I ate some custard today — I mean yesterday — and some soft-boiled egg."

"Good, honey!"

"But I wanted to ask you something, Alfie."

"What?"

I waited while she caught her breath. Even talking made her tired lately.

"It's about my crucifix," she said, so softly I could barely hear her.

"Oh."

"I think . . . I think I might be . . . I might be *need*ing it."

So that was it. That was what she wanted to talk to me about. The thing was, I really didn't know what else I could do about that. I had already written some letters, and I had even tried to phone this girl named Patti Peterson that I used to know in Van Nuys, but nothing had worked. I sent the first letter right after we moved here. I sent it to "Occupant" at our old address. I asked them to please remove the bottom drawer and send me the Jell-O box. But I never got an answer. Then I kind of forgot about it, because Francie didn't mention it for a long time. The next time she brought it up, she hinted that maybe Jesus was going to deliver it to her for

Christmas. So I wrote another letter. This time I asked the occupant to please write and give me their phone number, because this was *very important*. I was afraid to ask them to call me, because I didn't want to get a phone call about that crucifix when everybody was in the room and could hear me. The last thing I tried, I did just last year; I tried to find Patti Peterson. I was going to ask her to go get it for me. But she had moved, and I didn't know her father's name. I didn't know where she had moved to, and I didn't even know if it was Peter*son* or Peter*sen* or what. And now here was Francie, asking me for it.

Her arm was lying across the pillow. I was suddenly shocked by how thin it looked. She slowly moved it, covering her eyes with her hand.

"Alfie," she whispered, turning her face into the pillow, "tell me the truth. Did Jesus *really* give me that, or did you?"

I bent over her and put my mouth close to her ear. "What a question!" I whispered. Sometimes I amaze myself.

"Well, will you pray with me then?" she asked in a muffled little voice.

"Okay."

It wasn't a silent prayer. It was an out-loud one. Francie prayed it. I just can't repeat it. When I finally put the blanket up around her shoulders and left the room, I was a complete mess.

8

DAD AND I GOT A LATE START ON
Wednesday, the third day of the trial.
He spent a few extra minutes with
Francie before we left, and then he went to the bathroom for
quite a long time after that. I think he was crying. It's hard
to tell with my dad though, because of his glasses, and his
eyes look kind of bloodshot all the time anyway.

Even though I didn't really expect to see Kurt's bike parked
by the tree, I was still disappointed when it wasn't there. Up-
stairs, a little crowd was already gathered around the door of
the courtroom. We had to wait in a line in the hallway until
the bailiff came along and opened the door.

The main thing that happened in the courtroom that morning was that the defense, that is, the State of California, called
up this biophysicist from Berkeley, Dr. Jukes, who was the
author of the part of the Science Framework that the creationists were complaining about. Dr. Jukes said that the "Divine
Creation Theory" was excluded from the Science Framework because it was religious and supernatural, and, therefore,
not science.

When we broke for lunch, I just walked out of the court-room and turned right around and stood by the door. I was the first in line for the afternoon session.

I leaned against the wall and was watching all the people filing out of the monitor room when, suddenly, there he was!

He didn't see me at first, but as he walked past, his eye caught mine, and I could feel the blood suddenly rushing to my throat.

He looked really nice. He was wearing blue cords and a blue denim shirt under his jacket.

For a terrible moment I thought he might just keep walk-ing, but he hesitated for just a second and then made his way slowly through the crowd over to where I was standing.

"Hi. Still hanging in there, huh?" he said.

"Hiya Kurt!" I said, too enthusiastically, probably. "I didn't see you yesterday. Were you here?"

He shook his head. "No. Couldn't make it. Listen, I'm on my way to get something to eat. I thought I'd go find myself a milkshake somewhere." Then, as an afterthought, he asked, "You want to come?"

Of course, I realized that if I left with him, I would lose my place in line, but I could care less about that! Kurt was asking me out for a milkshake!

"Oh, I don't know," I said. "I'll lose my place in line."

Kurt shrugged.

"Unless," I added, "that is, unless I get a hot fudge sun-dae."

"Okay by me," he said. "Come on."

The corridor was busier than ever by then. Kurt grabbed my hand and pulled me along to the elevator. We got there just as the door was starting to close, but Ralph was there and when he saw us hurrying toward it, he kept the door from sliding shut and motioned for us to get aboard.

That was one strange elevator ride. I was pressed up really close to Kurt and I could feel his chin grazing the top of my head. The collar of his denim shirt was brushing against my face, and his neck smelled really nice. I mean, I'm no sex fiend or anything, I — well, anyway, my knees were starting to *melt*.

When we got down to the street floor, Kurt took hold of the back of my arm so we would stay together as we left the elevator. I was wondering if the ride had affected him too, or if I was just imagining things. I knew the answer right away though, because before he let go of my arm, he gave it a real hard squeeze — I mean, *really* hard — and he made this little growling noise way down deep in his throat.

That was one of the nicest things that ever happened to me. I'll probably remember it forever.

"I thought we'd go to that Country Maid, or whatever it is," Kurt said when we were out on the street. "I've got the car today. It's over in the lot over there. Or would you rather walk?"

"Oh, let's walk. We've got two hours."

Kurt shoved his hands in his pockets and we started off.

"Man, this case is really fizzling out," he said. "Those creationists." He made a little clicking noise with his tongue. "Those guys are really something else!" Then he added, "But they scare me too, you know? When they start fooling around with science — when they start pleading for *fairness* in the science class. . . ."

"Wait a minute now, Kurt," I interrupted, remembering how he had cut me down after we were interviewed on TV. "What's wrong with *fairness?*"

Kurt gave me an exasperated look. "Oh, Jesus," he said softly. "Do I really have to explain this to you?"

"Yes."

The light changed to green and we started to cross the street. Kurt reached out suddenly and grabbed me by the wrist. "Watch it!" he said, as this car came around the corner at about eighty miles an hour. But then, to my disappointment, he let go of my wrist and put his hand back in his pocket and we continued walking.

"Alfie," he said, "you may be surprised to learn that there are *not* two sides to everything. Some people still believe the world is flat, for God's sake. Other people believe that the moon-walk was done in a TV studio in the basement of the Pentagon. Do you want to be fair to them?"

"But wait a minute, Kurt! Creation and evolution are different! They're both just theories! Nobody knows for sure."

"How many science classes have you taken, Alfie?"

"What's that got to do with it?"

"How many?"

"Not many."

"Okay, can I tell you a little about science then?"

"Sure."

"You won't think I'm being — oh, I don't know. . . ."

"A pompous know-it-all?" I suggested.

Kurt grinned at me. "It wouldn't be the first time I've been accused of that, but this time I'll risk it. Okay, first of all, the test of a scientific theory is, can it be *dis*proven. Theories are theories until they've been *dis*proven. Then they're junked. So far, concerning evolution, that hasn't happened. Everything *fits*. See?"

"But what about creation?" I argued. "That hasn't been disproven either!"

"Two things," Kurt said. "First of all, science doesn't deal in the supernatural. The supernatural is outside the realm of science. The supernatural is religion's baby. Second, the difference between science — *real* science — and their so-called creation science is this," he said patiently, "science *starts* with little bits of information, little facts, and then comes up with a theory to explain them. In this case, the theory of evolution. Creation science, on the other hand, starts with a theory — the theory of creation, as written in Genesis — and *then* tries to find the facts to fit the theory. Do you see the difference? They're doing it backwards. You can see the difference there, can't you?"

"Well, sure. When you put it that way, but. . . ."

"Well then, you've got it. Listen, Alfie, I'm not against people thinking whatever they want to think. But not in the science class. Let them talk about creation in a comparative religions class or something like that. But in science class, we have to stick with the facts."

We got to the restaurant and Kurt swung open the door for me. "Want to sit at the counter?"

"Okay."

We climbed up on the stools, and Kurt pulled the menu from the little holder behind the napkins and opened it up in front of us. He leaned toward me. "This is on me," he said. "What would you like?"

"Just that hot fudge sundae you promised me. I'm on a diet," I smiled.

"You're crazy. You can't just have ice cream. You need some vitamins and some protein. How about a hamburger?"

"No. I couldn't eat a hamburger."

He looked at me.

"Really," I said. "I couldn't."

"Okay, we'll share one."

The waitress came by in a minute and Kurt told her we wanted the luncheon hamburger, which included a salad and fries, and when we finished that, a thick strawberry shake and a hot fudge sundae.

"Sorry," the waitress said. "Our hot fudge machine is on the fritz."

"Oh, no," I groaned softly.

"How about regular chocolate? Do you have that?" Kurt asked.

"Sure. We've got regular chocolate."

"Would that be okay, Alfie? A regular chocolate sundae?"

I nodded. "Sure. That's okay."

Kurt put his hand on my arm. "Sorry about that. About the hot fudge. I owe you one."

We got back to the courthouse just in time for the afternoon session. Judge Perluss said something really interesting that afternoon. He said that even if the State could *prove* the theory of evolution is true, we still have a First Amendment that guarantees free exercise of religion. He said that no matter what the scientists say, there are people that go home, open the Bible to Genesis and say, "This is the truth. This is the Word of God." And the judge said, "And they have a right to that belief!"

Kurt shook his head when he heard that. "They'll just have to keep away from science classes, I guess."

Finally, the judge recessed for the day. Kurt and I stood up and stretched a little.

"Going home now?" he asked.

I nodded. "Uh-huh."

"How about a ride?"

"Well, sure. That would be great."

Kurt has this cute yellow Toyota. And it was so *neat*. Most kids' cars are full of old cans and papers and garbage, but his was real clean.

I told him how to get to my street. "Which house?" he asked.

"That one. With all the cars around it. Oh, no! What day is it?"

"It's still Wednesday, I think."

"Wednesday Bible Study," I groaned.

Kurt pulled up in the driveway behind Pastor Huggins's old Cadillac.

"Well, thanks for the ride," I said. "And for the lunch. Thanks."

"You're very welcome."

I got out of the car, but before I shut the door, I stuck my head back in and said, "Well, so long, Kurt."

"Goodbye, Alfie."

I was waiting, but he didn't say one word about seeing each other again.

I went in through the back door, because I didn't feel like facing Pastor Huggins and the Wednesday Bible Study just then. I stopped in the kitchen and fixed myself a Coke, and then I went to my room through the back hall.

Aunt Marion was sitting at my desk reading one of my magazines.

"Hi, Aunt Marion." I dropped my backpack in the corner and took off my sweater and Levi's. Then I put on my sweatpants and gray Nike sweatshirt and collapsed on the bed.

Aunt Marion looked up from the magazine. "Want me to leave?"

"Doesn't matter."

"Hey, can I smoke in here?" she asked.

"No."

"Brat."

"How's Francie? Is she sleeping?"

Aunt Marion made a hopeless little gesture and shook her head. "She's resting. I don't know if she's asleep. Your mom wants to take her to see Brother Vinnie tomorrow night."

"Who's Brother Vinnie?"

"Dr. Vincent Prulain. He's giving a healing service." She jerked her head toward the front room. "When they started talking about it, I came in here. Everyone else thinks your mom should go. Belle Jorgenson said she has a *feeling* something wonderful will happen. So I left. I didn't want to say anything to upset your mother."

"You don't think they should go?"

"Of course not. Francie's in no shape to go anywhere."

I pulled my comforter up around my chin. "Maybe . . . maybe she'll get healed," I whispered, pulling up the comforter even higher.

Aunt Marion looked at me. "Yeah, maybe," she said, "but I'll not be any part of it. Don't be surprised tomorrow night if I suddenly get one of my famous migraines." She pushed the hair off her forehead. "You sure I can't smoke in here?"

"Come on, Aunt Marion. You know the rules. And when are you going to quit that filthy habit? And you a nurse, too."

"Is that right? Well, you're probably going to want a cigarette when I tell you what they've been up to out there."

"Who? What are you talking about?"

"The Wednesday Bible Study had an important item of business before they got to the subject of Brother Vinnie."

"So?"

"It was about Dungeons and Dragons."

I got up on one elbow. "What did they say about it?" I was interested because the Math Club has been playing D and D for almost a year.

"Dungeons and Dragons, my dear, comes straight from the hand of the devil. Millie Snyder heard on TV that one woman in the east was tossing her son's game into the garbage can, when she heard little muffled devil-screams coming from the plastic pieces. She slammed the lid of the can on quickly and ran to the house.''

"Aunt Marion, you're lying.''

She raised her right hand. "I swear to God. That's what Millie said. She said she couldn't vouch for it, but that's what she heard on TV.''

I stared at the ceiling. "Mrs. Snyder is crazy.''

"Maybe so. But I doubt if you'll be playing Dungeons and Dragons with the Math Club much longer.''

I ignored her. Pretty soon I said, "What else did they say?''

"Not too much about D and D. Just that they're going to form an action committee to spread the word. Alert people of the danger. Belle Jorgenson said a neighbor kid of hers told her that he plays the game after school — on school property.''

"My god,'' I said, "The kids in the Math Club play it all the time at school.''

"Well, they're going to see if they can put a stop to that. They're getting the rest of the members at church to write letters and so forth.''

"Gees!''

"And then they started talking about you.''

"What *about* me?''

"Well, about you and Mr. Burr, actually. Belle Jorgenson suggested to your mom that perhaps Mr. Burr wasn't such a good influence on you, and. . . .''

"*What?*'' I exploded.

"Listen, Alfie, don't get mad at *me!* I'm just telling you what they said. If you're going to get mad at *me,* I just won't say anymore.''

A typical Aunt Marion ploy. "Okay,'' I said. "I'm sorry. So what else did they say?''

"Well, Belle Jorgenson —''

"Belle Jorgenson is a narrow-minded bigot!" I interrupted.

"Tsk, tsk. Is that nice, Alfie? Anyway, Belle has been asking around, and now she's implying to your mother that she knows much more about Mr. Burr than she's able to repeat. She said she's afraid of some sort of retribution."

"Belle Jorgenson is also a pathological liar! I happen to know that for a fact! Remember that business last year when she accused poor Mr. Ryan of setting that fire in the church kitchen?"

"Well, at any rate, they phoned your school."

"They *what? * Who's *they?*"

"It was sort of a committee project you might say. As I recall, Pastor Huggins looked up the number, Mrs. Jorgenson dialed, and your mom did the talking. Somewhat reluctantly, I'll admit," she added.

"Who'd she talk to, for gods' sake?"

"Mr. Burr, I guess. He's the Math Club advisor, isn't he? And I think she told him you wouldn't be able to be his assistant anymore."

I could hear the meeting starting to break up in the other room. I just lay there on the bed, biting the inside of my cheek. That's a terrible habit I have that I've been trying to stop for years. Sometimes when I'm really upset, I'll bite so much that it starts to bleed.

"The others kind of talked your mom into it, honey," Aunt Marion said with unaccustomed gentleness. "You know how she goes along with whatever they say. Especially Pastor Huggins."

"Yeah. I know. But still! Now I'm going to have to have Dad call him back and everything." Dad was my old standby in cases like this. It didn't occur to me for one second that I would give up being Mr. Burr's assistant.

A few minutes later my mom came into my room. "Well, thank goodness that's over," she said, blowing a wisp of hair off her forehead. "They really seemed to enjoy that lemon pie though."

"Hey, Mom," I said softly, trying to control myself, "how come you phoned my school? And who'd you talk to, anyway?"

She glanced at Aunt Marion and her face flushed. "I'm . . . I'm sorry, dear. It's just that I didn't really have any choice in the matter. The others seemed so sure it was the correct thing to do. And Pastor Huggins said —"

"Who'd you talk to, Mom?" I interrupted.

"Well, I talked directly with Mr. Burr. I . . . I told him that due to some circumstances, you wouldn't be able to be his assistant anymore, and also that you wouldn't be able to play that Dungeons and Dragons game. The hand of the devil is truly —"

"Yeah, Mom, I know. But what did Mr. Burr say?"

"Well, as I remember, he said he was sorry to hear that, and he thanked me for calling."

That sounded just like Mr. Burr.

Mom came over to me then and put her arms around me. "I'm sorry, Alfie, really. I realize how much you enjoy being Mr. Burr's assistant, but I've simply got to do what's best for you, no matter how difficult it is. Don't you see?"

I didn't answer.

"And I am going to pray about it," she said. "I intend to pray very hard about it, and then do as the Lord directs."

Aunt Marion got up and started to leave the room. "I think I'll go check on Francie," she said.

Mom looked at her watch. "I'd better get dinner started."

She touched my shoulder. "Please, Alfie. Please try to understand."

Well, I could tell she was feeling bad about what she'd done, but still she had done it. And I couldn't imagine how she could go along with anything that crazy Belle Jorgenson said.

I went out on the chicken coop to watch the traffic on the freeway for a while and try to figure out what was going on. My mom said she intended to pray and do as the Lord directed. So what if I decided to do the same thing?

Right there and then I asked Jesus if I should remain as Mr. Burr's assistant. The answer came back so fast I couldn't believe it. So I asked again. The answer was still yes. So whose Lord did we follow? Mom's or mine?

I lay there on the roof for quite a long time just thinking about that. What was the good of those kinds of prayers if the answer could be different for everyone?

Pretty soon the wind came up, and I could feel it blowing my hair, parting it. Whenever I feel the wind parting my hair like that, I always think about Francie and one clear Easter morning long ago, when my mom and dad took us to a Sunrise Service way up on a high hill somewhere in Los Angeles. I was standing a few feet behind Francie, watching her fine golden hair in the early morning light as the wind kept parting it, gently exposing first one silky section, and then another. I don't think I can ever feel the wind in my hair without seeing Francie's head just as it looked that morning.

It was starting to get cold out there on the coop, so I got down and went back in the house. Mom was still busy in the kitchen, so I went back to my room and flopped on my bed and started to think about this monster pimple I had last year. I often wonder what kids with clear skin think about all the time in their moments of reverie.

I wrote a three-page composition in my English class a couple of weeks ago about that monster pimple. It was on my nose, on the left side of my nose, toward the front. Mr. Basil had assigned our Monday composition that week on the subject of health, so I wrote about the pimple. I had been wanting to tell someone about it for a long time anyway. But a monster pimple is not something you just start telling people about. Every week Mr. Basil reads the best composition to the class. Sometimes he picks mine. That week, however, he read Melissa Fontaine's. She wrote about abortion and amniocentesis, and about how nowadays women could choose *not* to have babies with certain diseases, and so forth. In Melissa's opinion, it was a great medical advancement. Most of the class seemed to agree.

Mr. Basil gave me a C over A. "Well written," he said, "but trite." That's all he knows.

Since my dad was eating out that night, we had baked fish for dinner. My dad hates fish, so Mom only cooks it when he's not home.

I was in a pretty bad mood and hardly spoke during dinner. Afterwards, Francie started asking me to play a game with her. She had had a late nap and was all hyper. Well, I really didn't feel like playing a game, but she started in on me like she does sometimes. She started getting all moody and whiny, so I said, "Oh, all right. What do you want to play?"

She said she wanted to play this old game we've had around the house for a million years called Barbie, Queen of the Prom. I don't know if they even make it anymore. It's one of those games that's so dumb, it's fun. In order to be Queen of the Prom, you have to get a boyfriend, a dress, and a club presidency. Well, I was lucky right away, and had the school club presidency and the dress before Francie got anything. And then she accidentally spilled the board and playing pieces and cards and everything all over the floor.

"What did you do *that* for?"

"It was an accident, Alfie."

I looked at her suspiciously.

"Honest! Let's start over again, okay?"

I was about to say no, but then Aunt Marion and Mom came into the room and I thought, Oh, what the heck. So we set it all up again. Luckily, Francie won it fair and square.

"Hooray!" she said. "Hey Mom! I'm Queen of the Prom!"

She wanted to play another game after that, but Aunt Marion wouldn't hear of it. "It's off to bed with ye, m'girl," she said.

I happened to glance at Mom as Aunt Marion was wheeling Francie out. I'll never, ever forget that look. Don't tell me about the suffering of Jesus on the cross.

After a while Mom got out her knitting and I went and put the dishes in the dishwasher and washed the pots. There weren't too many. Then I went back into the front room. Mom had put down her knitting by then and was just sitting, resting in her chair.

I sat down too. "Mom," I said quietly, after a minute, "you know, we were talking about amniocentesis in my English class the other day. You know, that test?"

"Yes. I know."

"Well, I was wondering, I mean, if you *knew* about—about how Francie would be — you know, before, well, would you. . . ."

"Have an abortion?" she asked gently.

I nodded. "Yeah."

My mom looked like she was about sixty years old. God, she looked tired. But she shook her head slowly, back and forth. "Of course not, Alfie," she said. "Francie is my child! I love her!"

My eyes filled with tears and so did Mom's.

I brushed my hand lightly under my nose and wondered what Melissa Fontaine would have thought of that.

9

SINCE MY DAD HAD AN EARLY DENTAL AP-
pointment Thursday morning, I had to take
the bus to the courthouse. I had trouble
finding my favorite blue jacket and thought I was going to
miss the bus. But I made it okay.

I kind of like taking the bus, it's so awful. The drivers are
usually really nice or really grouchy. That morning I had Mr.
Sunshine. That's what I call him. He's one of the grouchy
ones. Just for fun, I smiled and said good morning to him. It
really surprises him when I do that. Then I went all the way
to the back of the bus and scrunched way down in a seat by
the window, completely wrapped up in my old blue jacket.

A Mexican woman and her little boy were in the seat in
front of me, speaking Spanish. I had to smile, because it reminded me of when Mr. Burr showed the Math Club some
slides from his trip to Spain. It was after our regular meeting
last week.

Mr. Burr stood up with a big smile on his face. "I have
my famous slides of Spain with me this afternoon, about five

hours' worth, and anyone leaving the room at this time will do so at his own peril!''

"Hey, Mr. Burr," Clyde Jensen said, "I have to go to work!"

"Not good enough, Jensen," Mr. Burr replied sternly. The kids all laughed, and some of them left, but most of us stayed.

As he was setting up the projector, he told us how his wife had always wanted to go to Granada and see the Alhambra. So he started off with a picture of their *pension* in Granada, explaining how he had completed a six-week crash course in Spanish and knew the language completely.

"We were on a tight budget," he said, "so when the *señora* announced — in Spanish of course, since she knew no English — that the *pension* would only cost us the equivalent of six dollars a night, I became a bit rattled. The *señora* asked, 'How long will you be staying?' I shrugged and tossed off in my impeccable Spanish, '*Pues, dos años.*' The *señora's* eyes opened wide. '*¿Dos años?*' she asked, amazed.''

That's when, as Mr. Burr explained, his wife gave him a stiff sideways kick. "Dos días, you nincompoop!" she said.

My mom has always wanted to go to Europe. For a while there, after Aunt Marion came to live with us, it looked like my parents might actually go. I think my mom even went and saw a travel agent. But then they had some kind of argument and never discussed it again.

After the Mexican lady and the kid got off the bus, I just sat there and watched all the other people. Most people are sure funny-looking. I don't think I've ever seen a perfect human specimen on the bus. Come to think of it, I've never seen a perfect human specimen anyplace.

The way the people looked reminded me of Pastor Huggins' sermon a few weeks ago. He was talking about "glorified bodies." When the dead-in-Christ rise first, they will do so in glorified bodies. Heaven will contain only glorified bodies. Francie's body will be perfect.

The bus suddenly made a jolt. I looked out the window and noticed that half the cars on the road were full of dents and the road was full of potholes. The Bible says the streets of heaven are pure gold. The gates of heaven are made of pearl. It really does say that. I looked it up.

Not too long ago, the Answer Man Column in the newspaper asked people what they thought heaven was like. I cut out the article and put it in my shoebox. One guy said heaven was blue skies, no wind, and an empty court. A lady said, "Any place where Tony is." They were probably joking, though.

Suddenly, I thought about Alma Johnson. Was she really in heaven, waiting for Francie? When my mom suggested that, it sounded so right, my whole body tingled.

I thought about the Kingdom where no one grows old, where sickness and death are nonexistent, and where the lion lies down with the lamb. Just as I started to close my eyes, there on the bus, trying to envision such a place of perfection, I noticed that I had missed my stop. I got off the bus and had to walk back three blocks to get to the courthouse.

I was much too late to get into the real courtroom, so I went in and took a seat way in the back of the room with the TV monitor. I looked around, but I didn't see Kurt anywhere.

The State of California called some educators to the stand that day. One of them testified that the most important point in science is the absence of preset conclusions. "You are not out to justify," he said, "you are out to learn."

Another man said that the theory of evolution is based on a tremendous amount of data gathered over a long period of time. He said critics of evolution often dismiss it as "just a theory," but, he said, "In science, theories are powerful organizing concepts."

Most of the witnesses for the State that day sounded just like Kurt.

Late in the afternoon, when the judge finally adjourned for the day, I went and caught the bus home. When I got there, I walked around the side of the house toward the back door. There was my dad, dressed in his jogging suit, squatting by the back steps, squirting this dry spot on the lawn with the hose. The reason there's a dry spot on the lawn is because one of the sprinkler heads is broken and he hasn't replaced it yet. I guess he'd rather spend the time just watering it with the hose. My mom gets really irritated about that.

He looked up when he heard me. "Oh, there you are," he said. "Coming jogging with me today?"

Well, I knew I was going, because I wanted to explain to him how Mom had phoned up Mr. Burr and to ask him to make her phone him back or write him a note or something, and tell him she had changed her mind. I knew Dad would understand and see things my way when he heard the facts.

But even though I knew I was going to go jogging, I answered, "Well, *maybe*. Do you think I should?"

I was playing this little game we always played. Even though I hate going jogging, I like it too. I like it because it makes me feel really virtuous and thin, but I hate it because of the excruciating pain. So I always pretend I don't want to go, and I make up excuses.

I sat down on the porch step. "It *is* kind of windy." (Sometimes I say, "It *is* kind of cold," or, "It *is* kind of hot.")

Dad grinned at me. "It *is* kind of windy, that's true."

"But then, I didn't go yesterday."

"Or the day before."

"Well, I guess I could go, but you'd have to wait while I changed, and you probably wouldn't want to do that."

Just then the screen door opened slightly. "Watch out, Alfie," my mom said. "I'm coming out."

I scooted over to make room for the door to open. My mom stepped out on the little porch and stood there a few seconds. "Maybe you can stop by the hardware store this weekend and get a new sprinkler head for that," she said to Dad. "If you'll tell me the size and number, or however they come, I'll be more than happy to pick it up for you."

My dad just kept sprinkling the dry spot. "No thank you, Virginia," he said, ultra-politely. "I think I can take care of it myself, when I'm ready to."

I stood up. "Well, I guess I'll go change."

"Is this going to be a long job?" Mom asked. "When do you think you'll be back, Alfred?"

Dad looked up. "What difference does it make?"

"Well," Mom said, hesitating, "I . . . I have a favor to ask of you."

Dad just made kind of an exaggerated sigh.

"I'd like you to help me with Francie tonight. I want to . . . to take her out."

Dad looked incredulous. "Out? Are you crazy?"

Mom flushed. She touched her hair lightly with her hand, putting an invisible stray strand into place. "I want to take Francie to a special service tonight, Alfred. I need your help. That's not too much to ask, is it?" She paused. "After all, she *is* your daughter, too."

"Oh? Is that true? I wasn't aware of that." You could cut his sarcasm with a knife, as they say. I started to get a little stomachache then, and I should have gone inside, but something made me stay out there, some kind of weird perversion, like when I keep watching a certain sportscaster on TV, even though I can't stand the sight of him.

"Marion has a headache," Mom said, "and I can't handle Francie alone. But," she added softly, "I know I'm to take her there tonight." I noticed that my mom had the same mystical look on her face that she had the night she was telling me about Alma Johnson.

That's when this butterfly — maybe it was a moth, it was big and gray — flew right into the spray of water. My dad didn't even notice it. It fell in the mud just two feet from where I was standing. I watched it struggling for life. The more it struggled, the worse it was. It was burying itself in the mud.

"You *know* you have to take here there?" Dad mocked. "You *know* you have to take her there?" He shook his head in disgust. "Well then, I *know* you'll find a way." He went over and turned off the hose, and I went in the house.

Mom followed me in. I felt so sorry for her I couldn't stand it. Even though she had caved in to all that pressure from the Bible Study ladies and Pastor Huggins and phoned Mr. Burr and all that, I still felt sorry for her.

I stopped by the cupboard and got out a glass. I went to the refrigerator and poured myself a little Coke. "I'll go with you, Mom," I said at last. "I'll help you. What time does it start?"

Just then the doorbell chimed. I had made the doorbell myself from one of those Heathkit sets. You can fix it to play any tune you want. Right then it played the first seven notes of "All Things Bright and Beautiful." Francie had asked me to fix it to do that. She liked the program about the animals and that veterinarian in Yorkshire, and she liked the old hymn too —

All things bright and beautiful,
All creatures great and small,
All things wise and wonderful,
The Lord God made them all.

"I'll get the door, Mom," I said.

It was Tyler.

"Hi!" I said. "What's up?"

She stood to one side. "Ta-da!" she sang out, spreading her arms and pointing to her mom's car out by the curb.

"They let you *drive?*"

"First time, solo!" she said. "But they're sitting home biting their fingernails and watching the clock. I can only stay five minutes."

"Well, come in then," I smiled, "and talk fast."

"Hello, Tyler," Mom said, coming into the front room. Then she looked at me, and back to Tyler again. "Alfie, maybe Tyler would like to come along with us this evening."

I knew right away what Mom was thinking. She was thinking that in case we had to double-park or something, it would be a lot easier getting Francie out of the van with two of us doing it. That way, Mom could just stay in the driver's seat. I quickly explained the situation to Tyler. She thought about it for a second and said, "Oh, sure! Do you want to pick me up at home, or what?"

Mom looked at her watch. "We should leave within an hour. And we haven't had dinner. Could you stay for grilled cheese sandwiches, Tyler? Then drive yourself home when we get back?"

"Well, let me call home. If my mother doesn't need the car, that would work out okay."

Dad appeared in the doorway. "We'd better get going, Alfie. It's starting to cloud up."

I shook my head. "Oh, gee, Dad. I'm sorry. There's been a change in plans."

"The girls and I are having a quick bite and then we're leaving," Mom said coldly. "You and Marion will be on your own for dinner, I'm afraid."

My dad rolled his eyes toward the ceiling. "Oh, my!" he said. "I don't know if we can handle that."

Tyler laughed, embarrassed. She never quite knows how to act around my parents. I guess that's how it is with people from happy families. They just don't know how to act around miserable ones.

10

A N HOUR LATER WE WERE IN THE VAN ON
our way to the auditorium. It was just
starting to sprinkle, and the lovely odor
of spring rain filled the air.

"Who is Dr. Vincent Prulain, anyway?" Tyler asked
brightly. She was sitting up front with my mom. I was in back,
next to Francie, holding her hand.

"Well," Mom answered pleasantly, "Brother Vinnie is an
evangelist, a traveling evangelist. He comes up here to our
area about once a year." She paused and glanced at Tyler a
second. "He's truly one of the Lord's anointed. We're very
excited and hopeful."

Tyler didn't say anything more about Brother Vinnie after
that.

The sky let loose with a sudden torrent of rain when we
were about ten blocks from home.

"The windshield wiper's not working!" Mom said anx-
iously, pulling over to the curb. "I can't see a thing!"

She sat there and wrung her hands. "And I asked your father to replace those blades weeks ago!"

"Well," I said from the back, "it hasn't rained for quite a while."

"Now what do we do?" she asked impatiently. "I suppose we should find a phone and call your father." She looked at her watch and glanced back at Francie. "We'll be late for sure."

"Wait a minute," I said, rummaging around in the back of the van. "I think Dad keeps some spare blades here somewhere." I found them down in the spare tire well. "Ah, here they are!"

I wasn't sure how to change them, but it couldn't be too difficult. I started to get out of the car.

"Wait, Alfie," Mom said. "You'll get wet. Let me pull up under that tree."

She moved the car a little. "Do you know how to put those on?" she asked, with a touch of wonder in her voice.

"I'll figure it out," I said.

It took me a few minutes though. First I had to find out how the old ones came off, then I put the first replacement on backwards and had to do it over.

When I climbed back in the car, they all clapped. My Mom seemed genuinely amazed, but Tyler thought it was funny.

"That Alfie," Tyler said, poking me, "a real woman of the eighties. A future astronaut, for sure."

"I should say!" My mom said, missing the sarcasm as usual.

By the time we got to the auditorium, all the parking spaces for the handicapped were taken. Mom drove around the huge parking area, and then returned to the passenger loading zone near the entrance. Tyler and I got Francie out okay. Since she was shivering so much, I wrapped the extra blanket around her and put her little red wool hat on her head. Actually, in spite of the rain, it wasn't that cold an evening.

Mom rolled down the car window and told us she'd meet us inside. Her face was glowing.

An usher wearing a maroon jacket held open the door as I pushed Francie's wheelchair into the large lobby. It was crowded with people. Another smiling usher came up to us. "Good evening," he said. "We have a special wheelchair section this evening." His voice was soft and pleasant. He indicated the proper aisle. "Right down that way," he said.

"Thank you, but we have to wait for someone first."

"That's *per*fectly all right."

I knelt by Francie's side. "Doing okay, honey?"

"I think so, but where's Mom?"

"She'll be right here."

Tyler had wandered off a little way by herself. She went over to the bulletin board and looked around, and then came back again.

Pretty soon Mom walked in. It took her a minute to spot us in the crowd. "Oh, here you are!" she said cheerfully.

"They have a special wheelchair section," I said. I was so depressed I couldn't stand it.

"Well, that's wonderful," my mom said. "I'll meet you girls right here when it's over." She almost said something else. But then she smiled and bit her lip nervously and didn't say anything.

By now the music had started. It sounded like a piano and a small organ and a guitar. Mom smiled at Francie. "Ready?"

Francie said yes so softly I couldn't hear her. I could only see her lips move. I watched them start down the aisle toward the wheelchair section, Francie's head slightly tilted, as usual, and my mom, straightening her shoulders with a little shudder.

Oh, no, I thought, *I'm going to cry.*

Tyler turned toward me. "I can't get over it," she said quietly into my ear. "Everyone looks so *normal!*"

I blinked back my tears. "What did you expect?"

"I don't know. I thought they'd be different, that's all." Then she said softly, "Alfie, does your mother really . . . ?" She looked embarrassed and didn't finish her sentence.

"Let's go sit down," I said.

I recognized the song they were playing now —

> *I love to tell the story*
> *Of unseen things above,*
> *Of Jesus and His glory,*
> *Of Jesus and His love.*

All the aisle seats were taken, so Tyler and I had to file past several people in order to sit down. Everyone was so nice. Some people stood up so we could get by, and a couple of them smiled at us and said hello. Lots of them were singing along or humming with the music.

> *I live, I live, because He is risen,*
> *I live, I live to worship Him.*

They had a trio of singers on-stage, two women and a man. Most of the audience was singing along with them now. Some people were sitting with their eyes closed and their arms raised, hands slightly swaying.

Three men were standing on the stage, toward the side, and during the song they walked in and took their seats opposite the singers. I had never seen Brother Vinnie before, but I knew that he was in that group. I had been to enough healing services to know that.

"Is one of those guys Brother Vinnie?" Tyler whispered.

I nodded. I suspected he was the one in the middle. He had that *look* about him, for one thing, and his suit fit. Also, he was the only one sitting with his eyes closed and hands clasped together. The others were just looking over the crowd and smiling at their friends. They were obviously the local pastors.

"Probably the one in the middle," I whispered to Tyler.

If I leaned way over and looked past the heavyset lady in front of me, I could see Francie and my mom in the wheelchair section. I tried not to look at them.

Next to the heavyset lady was a young couple and their baby. The father was holding the baby. I think it had Down's syndrome. At least it looked like a picture of a baby with that disease that I had seen once. I tried not to look at them either.

I was right about which of the men on stage was Brother Vinnie, because pretty soon the guy in the middle got up and walked over to the microphone. It was the kind that was hooked on a tall stand, so you could unhook it and walk around with it. It had a real long cord and he could practically go from one end of the stage to the other.

Now they were singing, "Hallelujah! Hallelujah! Lord, I thank you," and Brother Vinnie was singing along with them. Then the trio started humming softly and Brother Vinnie was saying in a kind of monotone, "Lord, I praise you. Oh, Lord, I thank you," over and over and over. Then he got up real close to the microphone and whispered, "He's *here!* People, He's *here!* Can you feel His Mighty Presence?" A slight murmur flowed through the audience. A man down in front suddenly stood up and started speaking in tongues. Then several others scattered throughout the audience did the same.

Tyler poked me. "What's going *on?*" she whispered. "Let's get *out* of here!" she said, trying to be funny.

After a few minutes, Brother Vinnie held the microphone out at arm's length and just shouted in a loud voice, "How many in this room want God's best for this evening? Raise your hands!"

Hands flew up all around us, along with a mighty roar. Tyler looked at me in amazement. I tried to ignore her. Actually, she was starting to bug me a little.

"Oh, *people!*" Brother Vinnie said, "Ain't the devil gonna be glad when *this* is over!" There were shouted amens and a scattering of applause and laughter. "But first we're going to make him *suffer* tonight! Oh yes, people, but oh, listen! I have placed my family in financial jeopardy because of this ministry! But we want to see *thousands* turn to Christ — we want to see *young* people turn to Christ! And we will! But, oh people, how the price of everything is going up, and up, and up! We need your help, and we need it now! I'm believing in God for a *financial miracle* tonight!"

The ushers in their maroon jackets suddenly appeared in front of the auditorium, two for each aisle. They started the collection plates going as Brother Vinnie continued, head bowed, eyes closed, "I pray that some businessman will invest in the *Lord* tonight! I pray for a *thousand* dollars from someone in this audience tonight! Talk with the Lord, people! Is it you? Answer His call! Quickly, quickly! Oh, oh! There's a *mira*cle happening right *now.*"

The plate passed on down the row to Tyler. Neither one of us had a purse or any money. As she passed the plate to me, she leaned over and said softly, "He sure doesn't waste any time!"

Her comment surprised and shocked me. They always pass the plate before a healing service. I saw nothing unusual about that at all.

The trio had started singing again as the collection plates

made their rounds. Brother Vinnie kept talking into the microphone. "We'll give Him *all* the glory — He alone is worthy. We'll give the glory to *God.*"

The trio finished the song and the collection was over. Brother Vinnie thanked the trio and they went and sat down. I avoided looking at Tyler.

Then Brother Vinnie talked for a while about some of his personal experiences — his childhood, his alcoholic mother, his absent father. But he came through it all because he found the Lord during a service not unlike this one. He had come to scoff, but, by golly, when he left, he was *saved!* Hallelujah!

Slowly the lights began to dim. Brother Vinnie spoke even closer into the microphone. "I feel *Je*sus all over this building." There were more murmurs. "Close your eyes! Close your eyes, people, and let's just wait on *God!*"

I closed my eyes. It was as quiet as a tomb. Then Brother Vinnie started again in a soft, low voice. "There are those here, Lord, who need *healing* tonight."

Oh, Francie, I thought, *if only.*

"The glory will be yours, oh Lord," Brother Vinnie intoned. "Oh, people, you are not in this room tonight by *accident!* Don't you think *for one moment* that you are in this room by accident! You are in this room because God Almighty has placed you here! God has a plan for you, and He is working it out. My friends, the Lord Himself has led you here."

Could it be? Could that be true?

The trio started humming again, the organ softly playing. "But oh, my God!" Brother Vinnie said. "There is something holding us back! The spirit of God wants to *move* in this room tonight, but that old devil — that old devil Satan is

124

hanging on — hanging on for dear life! Out!" he shouted. "Out, you coward devil!"

That's when I started to go a little crazy. It was like I was building this house of cards, stacking and balancing one flimsy card on another, building a tower of cards, with me floating in the air at the very top of the tower. I *knew* my unbelief was keeping something wonderful from happening in that room. If I could just break through — crack through that wall of unbelief — miraculous things would happen. Francie would rise from that chair and come to me. "Look!" she would shout. *"I'm walking! I'm healed!"*

"Jesus is knocking!" Brother Vinnie intoned. "Let Him in! Let Him in! This is a Tabernacle of the Holy Spirit! There is something *mighty* in this room! Do you feel it? It's all over your body, like warm oil. The pain is leaving! The affliction is leaving your body! Oh, hallelujah!"

His voice was filled with urgency and excitement. "I don't understand it!" he said, "But get up! Get up as soon as you know it! Oh, thank you, thank you, thank you *Jesus*!"

A feeling of power and euphoria raced through my body. I had broken through! My eyes were still closed. I put my head in my hands; I was dizzy with power. At that moment, I knew I could do anything. I could say the word, and Francie would be healed. *She is going to get well!* I knew it! I could feel it!

"Move to the aisles *now*, as soon as you know you are healed! There is a woman with phlebitis — she's over there, way in the back! Come forward! You are healed! Come, people! Come! The Lord will not multiply his miracles until you come forward and acknowledge Him. The Lord will not give us a new miracle until His fruit is collected!"

People started straggling up to the stage, a few at first, then more and more. "Thank you, Lord!" Brother Vinnie shouted. "Let's give the Lord a clap offering!"

Tyler leaned forward and touched me on the knee. "A *clap* offering?" she asked, with an incredulous expression. "My God!" And then she started to laugh.

I think, at that moment, I actually hated her.

I looked at the stage. It was filling with people. The ushers would speak to them for a few seconds, and then sort of line them up on the stage, in separate little groups. Brother Vinnie hurried over to one little group of them. "Tell me, tell me quickly," he said to the first man in line. "How has God healed you?" There were some unintelligible murmurings into the microphone. Brother Vinnie spoke into it again. "Spasms! Your chest spasms are gone! Hallelujah!"

The audience echoed, "Hallelujah!"

Brother Vinnie was in a frenzy. I stood up to see if I could see Francie, but there were too many people crowded around the wheelchair section. I couldn't see her anymore.

Brother Vinnie raced to the other side of the stage, trailing his long cord. "Quickly!" he said. "How has the Lord healed you?" A large black woman grabbed the microphone out of his hand. "The lump is gone!" she said. The audience went wild. "Praise the Lord!" Brother Vinnie shouted. "I claim no glory! Glory be to the *Lord!*"

The place was a madhouse. People were getting healed all over the stage, and more were hurrying down the aisles. "Satan, I bind you, in the name of *Je*sus! There is a damaged nerve in the knee. It's cured! There is a person here, suffering from asthma for twenty years. Where are you?" Brother Vinnie held the microphone in front of a lady who was standing on crutches. She suddenly dropped the crutches and hugged Brother Vinnie. The audience cheered and stomped.

I was still in a daze. I kept looking for Francie and my mom on the stage. I was still somewhere up in the air, weightless, precariously swaying and floating above my house of cards.

Brother Vinnie suddenly pointed to where we were sitting. "Someone is healed over there, in that far section!"

No, I thought, panicked and confused. *Not here! Not me! It's Francie! Point to Francie!* But he kept pointing over to us. "Someone is going to be healed of a terrible affliction! You know who you are! Come! Come!"

The kid sitting next to Tyler suddenly stood up. He was about eighteen, and he had the worse case of pimples I ever saw. His face was a mask of welts and blisters, but his eyes were glazed over with hope.

He quickly made his way past Tyler, but as he was crossing in front of me, he stomped hard on my foot, crushing it with his black cowboy boot. It hurt so much I couldn't believe it. I guess that's what first snapped me out of my trance, or whatever you want to call it.

But it was what Tyler said a second later that *really* brought my illusionary house of cards tumbling down all around me. She tugged at my sleeve as the pimply-faced kid headed toward the healing platform. "Alfie!" she said. "Hey Alfie! I'll bet you a million bucks Jesus doesn't do acne!"

I bent my knee and brought my aching foot up to the edge of my seat. Then I slipped off my shoe and cradled my foot in my hands.

I watched as the poor kid climbed to the stage. An usher whispered to him for a minute or two, and then directed him toward the back of the platform, to a section of the stage Brother Vinnie was leaving strictly alone.

"See how he does it?" Tyler whispered fiercely. "What a

sham! The ones they can't *cure*," she said derisively, "they send over there! What a bunch of disgusting crooks! Look what he *heals* — chest spasms and arthritis!"

Brother Vinnie, meanwhile, was still doing his stuff. "Your lower intestinal trouble," he said to a fat lady in red slacks, "your lower intestinal trouble is cured!" He grabbed a little girl by the hand. "Your scoliosis is gone! Oh, praise the Lord! You've been wearing a brace for it, haven't you, honey? But now you can take the brace off! Throw it away! Oh, give the glory to *Jesus*!"

Brother Vinnie suddenly and dramatically put his hand to his head and paused a moment. Then he started talking softly and deliberately. "There is a parent who has brought a child here tonight." The couple in front of us glanced at each other quickly and then moved to the edge of their seats. The woman half stood, and the man held the baby out, like an offering. "This baby," Brother Vinnie continued, "is suffering from a *serious* illness. But nothing is too difficult for our Lord!" The audience cheered, but then a breathless hush fell over the auditorium. Suddenly, Brother Vinnie looked up into the balcony directly above us. "Your child is healed!" he shouted.

"Praise the Lord!" someone shouted.

"Amen!"

"Amen!"

The couple in front of us turned and stared up into the balcony behind us. I'll never forget the look of surprise and dismay on the woman's face. Then the man turned and slumped down in his seat. The woman buried her head in her hands.

Tyler looked at me. There were tears in her eyes. "Let's go," she said. "Let's go wait in the lobby."

I slipped my shoe back on and limped after her without a word.

Several people were standing around in the lobby, obviously bored and impatient. One guy looked like my father. That's what he used to do whenever my mom talked him into going to a healing service, wait in the lobby with the rest of the unbelievers.

Tyler touched my hand. "Alfie, are you okay?"

I had a splitting headache and I could barely stand on my bad foot. "Yeah," I said. "I'm okay."

I guess Tyler knew I didn't feel like talking. We found a bench to sit on, and we just sat there quietly until the service was over. I was watching one of the ushers set up a table where they were going to take orders for tapes of this evening's proceedings and sell Brother Vinnie's new book, *How I Found God in a World of Sin.*

I dreaded seeing Mom and Francie. I knew Mom would have that undaunted smile pasted on her face, as always. Pretty soon they came out. We stood up and waited for them to come over to us. Mom looked pale and drained, but that brave, patient smile was still on her face, just as I had expected. "Wasn't he *won*derful!" she exclaimed.

Tyler smiled a sick little smile. I think Tyler thinks my mom is nuts.

Francie's eyes were red with unshed tears. I bent down to her and put my cheek against hers for a moment. She brought her hand up slowly and patted my face.

"You know what, Alfie!" she asked, glancing up at Mom.

"What, baby? What is it?"

She tried vainly for a smile, but couldn't quite manage it. "It's my canker sore," she started, looking up at Mom again. "I . . . I think it's better!"

She moved her mouth around a little. "Yes! It really is! My canker sore is really better!"

I looked up just then and saw Brother Vinnie standing by the table with his books and things. He was shaking hands and autographing his book. I wanted to go over and strangle him.

11

FRIDAY, THE WORST DAY OF MY LIFE, started out like any other day — Mom and Dad ignoring each other at breakfast, and me pretending not to notice, making conversation with first one, then the other. Mom cooked sausages and pancakes, and Dad scanned the morning paper and just picked at his breakfast.

I didn't say anything about Mr. Burr right then, of course. I didn't want to discuss Mr. Burr in front of Mom.

I looked in on Francie before we left. She was lying in bed, only half-awake, but her eyes opened wide when she saw me bending over her.

"Came to tell you goodbye," I whispered. "I'll see you this afternoon, okay?"

A smile flickered across her face. She started to say something, but she had to clear her throat first. "Do you . . ." she started weakly, "do you think my crucifix . . . ?" She looked away for a minute, just with her eyes, without turning her head. Then she started over. "I mean, I really *want* it, Alfie!"

I could tell she was trying hard not to cry.

I bent down and kissed her. "I'll get it for you," I lied. "Don't worry now."

"You promise?"

I nodded. "Okay. I promise."

She blinked hard once or twice, and smiled.

"Be a good girl," I said, "and I'll see you later."

"Okay, Alfie."

Dad had to get some diesel fuel that morning on the way to the courthouse. I sat in the car, waiting. I couldn't get the picture of Francie out of my mind.

As he was getting back in the car, Dad said, "Hey, let's stop in at Denny's. You want some hot chocolate?"

I looked at my watch and sighed. I was probably too late to make the line for the real courtroom and I'd have to go in the TV monitor room anyway, so I said, "Sure."

We sat at the counter at Denny's and Dad ordered a sweet roll and a cup of coffee. I couldn't believe it. Mom had just fixed him a real breakfast, and he didn't even eat it.

"They'll probably wind up that creation trial today," Dad said, stirring his coffee.

"Yeah. I guess so." I decided that now was probably a good time to tell him about Mr. Burr. "You know," I said, "I'm having some trouble with Mom."

"Join the club, honey," he said, without even a hint of a smile.

"Well," I continued, "she has some idea that I shouldn't be Mr. Burr's assistant anymore." I looked at him to see if he was listening. Sometimes I'll tell him something and find out later that he wasn't even listening.

He was listening this time. "Why not?"

"It all started at Bible Study, I guess. Someone started complaining about how we play D and D at school."

132

"D and D?"

"Dungeons and Dragons. You know. Well, what finally happened was, Mom phoned up Mr. Burr at school and told him I couldn't be his assistant anymore."

"Because of that game, or what? I don't get it."

"Yeah, well see, Mom thinks it's some kind of a devil's game, and she doesn't want me playing it, or associating with Mr. Burr, because he's the Math Club advisor and —"

Dad was *really* paying attention now. He kept watching me very closely, sliding his fingers around his hairline like he always does. "Your mother has some problems, Alfie. You know that, of course."

"Yeah."

He poured some sugar into his spoon and then held it flat on the surface of his coffee, letting the coffee attack the sugar in the spoon. When the sugar was all brown with coffee, he let the spoon slip all the way into the cup. We both sat there and watched it as if it were the chemistry experiment of the century.

"Okay," he said finally. "I'll take care of Mr. Burr. I'll call him or something."

I was really relieved. "Thanks a lot, Daddy."

He sighed wearily and stirred his coffee some more. "About that game now, how many kids usually play?"

"What?"

"D and D. How many kids are involved with it?"

"Oh, I don't know. Half a dozen or so. It's just some of the kids in the Math Club."

He didn't say anything for a few minutes. I watched the cook slide platters full of eggs and hash-browns onto the high counter for the waitresses to puzzle over. They'd check their little pads and then look at all those plates of food, rejecting some, taking others, until they had an armful.

"You really enjoy it — playing this game, I mean?"

I nodded. "Uh-huh. There's really nothing *wrong* with it, Dad. It's just a fantasy game, you know. And we use lots of math. It's fun. It's just a *game*."

"Yes. I know. I know it's just a game. But the thing is, it really puts me in a tough spot, having to overrule your mother all the time."

"Well, but still, she's so —"

"What did she say about it, *exactly?* What did she say was wrong with it?"

"It was Pastor Huggins who did most of the complaining about it, at Bible Study on Wednesday. Aunt Marion told me he said it was inspired by the devil or something. Mom just goes along with whatever he says."

"I see."

"Aunt Marion told me some crazy stuff about how Pastor Huggins believes some story about how the plastic pieces were screaming or something when some lady back east threw them in the garbage can."

Dad was looking at me in this really funny way. "What did you say?" he asked, as if he didn't get it straight. "The plastic pieces were screaming, or the lady?" and I started laughing, and then he started laughing, too. I think we got a little hysterical. We just sat there at the counter, bent over with laughter, tears spilling from our eyes.

Finally Dad got out his wallet. He put a quarter on the counter. "Come on. I've got to get to work."

I suggested he just drive to his office and park in his regular place and I'd walk from there to the courthouse. It was a nice day, and I wasn't in any big hurry.

I was right about being too late for the real courtroom, anyway. They hadn't opened the door yet, and the line was a mile long. I guess those people didn't know that only twenty-four of them would get in.

I walked into the TV monitor room and took a seat way in the back. A second later, Kurt suddenly swung into the seat beside me and touched my arm.

"Hi, there," he said. "I was beginning to think you wouldn't be here today."

Just seeing him there, so suddenly like that, took my breath away for a second. The way he had talked on Wednesday about how the case had "fizzled out" had made me think he wouldn't bother about coming anymore.

I think I was blushing. At least I felt like I was.

"Hi, Kurt."

Gees, he looked nice. Those clear, bright eyes and that curly hair that I always wanted to touch and that nice neck. Ever since that little incident in the elevator, I couldn't forget about Kurt's neck.

I took off my blue jacket and hung it on the back of my seat. I didn't have my backpack that day, I just had this old shoulder-strap leather purse that Aunt Marion gave me when I started high school.

Kurt sat there with his arms crossed, watching me get all settled.

"So," he said finally, smiling at me.

"So," I answered.

"So, what have you been up to? Did you come to the trial yesterday?"

"Yeah. It was interesting. They had all these scientists and educators trying to explain what science is. They all sounded like you," I added.

Kurt laughed gently. "Oh, yeah?" He reached down and zipped open his orange backpack. "I brought you something,'' he said, and handed me a book. "I'll want it back, though. It's my grandfather's.''

He'll want it back! That meant he'd have to see me again. He'd have to see me again after the trial, to get his book back!

I swallowed and tried to sound normal. "What is it?''

"Ingersoll's Greatest Lectures. Ever heard of good old Colonel Bob?''

I shook my head. "No.''

"Well, I didn't think so. Robert G. Ingersoll, America's Beloved Infidel. I think you'll find the old colonel *veerry* interesting.''

"Gee, thanks.''

The bailiff suddenly shut the door. We looked at the TV monitor. Judge Perluss was entering the courtroom. He took his seat behind the bench.

My dad was right about that being the last day of the trial, because that's just what the judge said. He said he wanted to finish up that day.

The next half-hour or so was filled with lawyer talk. I was slumped way down in the chair with my head resting on my jacket, when I suddenly felt someone tapping me real hard on the shoulder. I shot up, startled. It was Aunt Marion. She was leaning over Kurt and motioning insistently toward the door.

I stood up quickly, holding my purse and the Ingersoll book.

"What is it?'' Kurt whispered, half rising.

"I don't know,'' I whispered back. But I think I knew. I followed Aunt Marion out to the corridor. She looked terrible. She was wearing her old raincoat and her hair was all wind-blown. Her eyes were puffy and red.

She put her hand on my shoulder and said, "It's Francie. I'm double-parked. We've got to hurry.'' She grabbed my hand and pulled me to the elevator.

"What happened?" I asked, tripping along behind her, trying to keep up.

Aunt Marion didn't answer until we were in the elevator. "She's going, Alfie. Dr. Amos is there."

The elevator door opened and we rushed out. "She'll probably be dead by the time we get there," Aunt Marion said, in her usual blunt way.

I didn't believe her. It just made me mad hearing her say that. "Who said that?" I demanded. "Did Dr. Amos say that?"

Aunt Marion shook her head. "Come on. The car's in front."

She had brought the van. The meter maid's little wagon was parked alongside it; she was writing out a ticket.

I got in on the passenger side and Aunt Marion ran around to the driver's side. The meter maid was standing in back of the van now, copying down the license number.

Aunt Marion rushed up to her. "Give me that damn thing!" she said. "A little girl is dying! Hurry up and give me that damn thing!" She snatched the ticket right out of the meter maid's hand and climbed into the van. "Damn meter maid!"

"Who said she's dying?" I asked again as we were speeding along the freeway.

"Come on, Alfie, nobody has to *say* it!"

"Is Daddy there?" I thought I was going to throw up.

"He should be, by now. Your mother phoned him. We thought it would be easier if I just came for you."

I had never seen Aunt Marion drive so fast. But it seemed like that five-minute trip took five hours.

I knew we were too late as soon as we got in the room. My father was bent over the bed, his head buried in the pillow next to Francie's; and his hands were holding hers — his two hands holding one of hers. He was sobbing into the pil-low.

Dr. Amos was standing nearby, looking grim, filling out some kind of form. My mom was next to him, gazing out the window. She looked up when we came into the room. There was no sign of tears, only her gentle, hypnotic smile. "Francie is all right, Alfie," she said. "She is all right at last. Francie is with the Lord."

And then something really terrible happened. That gentle smile just sort of froze on her face for a second, and then her whole body started to collapse. I rushed over to her just in time and took her in my arms. She buried her face in my shoulder and started to sob.

12

I DON'T EXACTLY REMEMBER WHAT HAP-
pened next, except that I kind of wandered
around the house for a while, crying in cor-
ners. Once my dad asked me if I wanted to go in and tell her
goodbye. I said no. I thought that would be useless. And then,
pretty soon, they came and took her away.

Not long after they did that, the people started arriving —
and the food. I guess what happened was that Aunt Marion
phoned Millie Snyder, and Millie Snyder phoned everyone else.
They were mostly people from church, friends of my mom.
And they seemed to be a great comfort to her. *"Francie is
with the Lord. Praise the Lord! Francie is with the Lord.
Hallelujah!"* You could almost see her faith strengthened and
renewed with each new arrival. And the casseroles started to
pile up in the refrigerator.

But I was just wishing everyone would go away and leave
us alone. When I couldn't stand it anymore, I went to my
room and shut the door. Once Dad came in and told me that
old Mrs. Thompson wanted to speak to me, but I wouldn't

come out. After a while — I don't know how long — he came around again and knocked and called out to me. I got up from my bed and opened the door.

"Let's get out of here," he whispered. "Let's go for a ride or something."

I dried my eyes and blew my nose and all that. "Okay."

"Shall we ask Marion to come along?" he asked.

"Okay."

So the three of us went for a ride along the river. After driving along silently for a few minutes, my dad sighed heavily and said, "Well, it's over."

I looked out the window. "Yeah," I said.

Aunt Marion said the river sure looks nice this time of year. She also said she planned to move out in a day or two, right after the funeral. She had recently run into an old friend from nursing school, newly divorced, and the two of them were going to try sharing an apartment. And Dr. Amos had mentioned something about a nursing position opening up in his office.

"Well, that's fine," Dad said. And then he added, "I don't know what we'd have done without you, Marion, these past few years."

Aunt Marion just nodded. "Thanks, Al." She got out her handkerchief and blew her nose. "She was a darling child."

That's when I started crying the most, there in the back seat. Pretty soon Dad stopped the car and we all got out. I went off by myself and sat on the ground and looked at the river.

I looked at the river for a long time, watching the leaves floating down the water with the current. I watched how some of the leaves just kept sailing along for as long as I could see them, swirling through little whirlpools and navigating among the fallen, rotting logs. But lots of other leaves got stuck. Some of them got caught on the brush along the bank of the river, and there they stayed, their journey ended. I closed my eyes and pretended I was one of those leaves in the water. I felt myself being carried along the current, helpless, but calm. I was a floating leaf, calm and accepting. Would I make it through the torrent or would I be snagged by an overhanging branch, twirled for a moment and stopped forever? I didn't care. The leaves didn't care, and neither did I.

"Alfie? Alfie?" It was my dad. "Are you ready to go?"

I got up and brushed the dirt and grass off my jeans. "Yes," I called back. I'm ready."

Gregg was waiting for me when we got home. He gave me a great bear hug, and I felt his big body moving with quiet sobs. I patted his shoulder. "It's okay, Gregg," I whispered. "It's okay."

After a while we went out in the back and sat on the coop, our legs dangling over the edge of the weather-beaten roof, just like when we were kids.

"Your mom is taking it really well," Gregg said.

I nodded. "We've all had lots of time to prepare."

"Yeah. That's true, I guess. But still, it's never easy."

Gregg pulled a handkerchief from his back pocket and blew his nose. "It's . . ."

He sighed and was quiet for a few minutes. We just sat there listening to the birds chirping away.

Then he tried again. "Francie's soul is in perfect hands now." He turned his head, and I could see the tears glistening in his eyes.

I hesitated. "Yes," I whispered.

"I had a chance to talk to your mother, you know, just before you got back. She told me she could almost *see* her little girl sitting at the feet of our Lord."

Gregg leaned back on the palms of his hands and looked up into the trees. "And that's a wonderfully comforting thought."

I reached up and picked a leaf off the eucalyptus tree. The branch sprang back toward the sky as the leaf came off in my hand. "Yes, it is a comforting thought," I said. And then I added softly, "If you believe it. But Gregg," I asked, touching his hand, "is it true?"

"Well, I think it's true, Alfie," he said gently. "And thinking it's true is the important thing."

I put my hands between my knees and rocked rhythmically from side to side. That was the most pitiful statement I had ever heard in my life. It was so pitiful, I couldn't even answer it.

Gregg was staring down at his feet now. His canvas shoes were starting to come apart on the outer edges, and he was bending his toes and looking at the holes in his shoes, watching them turn from little slit holes to round circle holes. I dropped the leaf and watched it sail to the ground.

"You know, Gregg," I said finally, "I'm having trouble trying to figure out why an all-powerful God would create a person like Francie just to make her suffer and die."

"Well, I don't know what God had in mind," Gregg said, "but He had a purpose." His voice softened. "And besides, she had happy times, too, Alfie. You know she had some happy times."

I suddenly felt very tired. "Well, maybe she did," I admitted, "but she suffered a lot too, Gregg. And I don't mean just physically, either. She suffered mentally, too. Boy, she wanted to get out of that wheelchair so bad, and walk, and roller-skate —"

"You know what, Alfie?" Gregg's face crinkled up into a

determined smile. "I'll bet she's walking and roller-skating now! I'll bet she's roller-skating with the Lord!"

The roof of the chicken coop felt hard and cold under me. I swung my legs and kicked the side of the little building with my heels. I kicked it over and over, and harder and harder.

"Gregg," I said finally, "I find that very difficult to believe."

I jumped down from the coop and looked toward the house. "I haven't eaten all day. I've got the shakes."

Gregg jumped down heavily and landed at my side. But as I started to walk back to the house, he reached out his hand and touched my shoulder.

"Alfie," he said. "Wait. I want to tell you something."

His eyes glistened and he looked as if he could hardly contain his excitement.

"What? What is it, Gregg?"

"I've finally made up my mind, while you were out with your dad — you know — I was thinking about it for a long time, but now I'm sure of it."

I looked at him, just waiting, hoping that he wasn't going to say something stupid — like he loved me or something.

"I'm going to be a minister, Alfie!"

Suddenly I felt just like I was in the movies. It was thrilling, that's all, like in one of those old movies I see on TV sometimes with Spencer Tracy or Pat O'Brien or James Cagney, all those old guys. These two kids grow up together and then one of them decides he's going to be a priest or something, and the other one usually ends up being a gangster, but even so they remain special friends all through their lives. Well, I didn't intend to be a gangster, of course, but I knew then that Gregg and I — in spite of all our differences — would be special friends forever.

"Oh, Gregg," I whispered, "that's *great*. Really. I'm so happy for you." I impulsively kissed him on the cheek. "You'll be a wonderful minister. I know it."

He gave me a playful little punch in the ribs. "Come on," he said. "My mom brought over an enchilada casserole. Let's go have some."

Aunt Marion was fussing around in the kitchen. "Hi, kids," she said. "Can I fix you something? I don't know if we're eating formally, all together, or not. But you really should have something to eat, Alfie." I had never heard her voice so gentle.

I sat down and Gregg went to the refrigerator and brought out a quart of milk and then he got two glasses from the shelf. I could hear my mom saying goodbye to someone at the front door. A minute later she came into the kitchen.

"They're all gone," she said. "Except for Millie, of course."

Mom sat down with Gregg and me at the table. "I called your grandparents, Alfie. The funeral's not till Monday, but they're flying into San Francisco in the morning. We're all going to pick them up. Would you like to come?"

For one awful moment I pictured myself riding in a car all the way to San Francisco and back with my mom and dad and Aunt Marion. "No. No thanks, Mom," I said. "I'll just wait for you here."

"What time's the plane coming in?" Gregg asked.

Mom checked a scrap of notepaper. "Eight thirty-four. We've got to get an early start."

"I'll come over and keep you company in the morning, Alfie," Gregg said, just as his mom walked in the room.

"Yes, Gregg," Mrs. Snyder nodded. "That would be nice."

I shrugged. "It doesn't matter. But if you want to." Then I said, "I think I'll call Tyler."

I love old Tyler. I really do. She wanted to come over right then, but I told her I was fine. "We're going to eat in a few minutes anyway," I said. "You can come over in the morning though, if you want. Unless you have other plans."

"Don't be silly," she said. "I'll be over in the morning. And Alfie, I'm really sorry. I just don't know what else to say."

"Yeah, I know," I said. "It's okay. I'll see you tomorrow."

Aunt Marion went out in the yard and found Dad watering the dry spot, and then they came in and we all had something to eat. I was glad Gregg and Mrs. Snyder were there. They really kept the conversation going. Gregg was kind of funny, actually. He kept sampling all the casseroles; he just stood at the refrigerator, with the door open, sampling casseroles.

"Is that one any good?" I asked, after he had taken three or four huge bites of something in a Pyrex baking dish.

"I don't know yet," he said with his mouth full, and we all laughed, his mom beaming, leading the chorus, proud that her son was cheering up the bereaved little family.

After dinner, I excused myself and went and took a bath so hot I could hardly stand it. I lay there in the tub and let the hot water keep running in a tiny trickle until the whole bathroom was filled with steam. After a while I shut off the faucet with my foot and stuck my big toe in the spout, or spigot, or whatever you call it. I've been doing that ever since I've been big enough to take baths by myself. And every time I do it, I wonder what would happen if I got my toe stuck in there. I've probably wondered that 4,315 times. And I've also wondered if I used up new brain cells every time I worried about that, or if I just kept using the same old ones every time. And this time, I had a new thought. I thought, *This is the first time I've stuck my toe in the bathtub spigot since*

Francie died. So this time, it's different. Everything I do, from now on, will be different.

After my bath, I put on my pajamas and robe and decided I might as well go to bed. There was nothing else to do anyway. Mrs. Snyder and Gregg hadn't gone home yet, so I went in and told them goodnight. Mrs. Snyder got up from her chair — they were still all in the kitchen — and came over and hugged me. That was a really surprising thing for her to do, because as I said before I really don't think she likes me very much. And it was funny, because then all the rest of them had to hug me, too. I guess my mom and dad figured it would look funny if Mrs. Snyder hugged me and they didn't.

I went right to my room and got in bed and turned off the light. For a long time I lay there, alone in my room, listening to what was going on in the house. The kitchen noises continued for a while, and finally I heard the front door close. Mrs. Snyder and Gregg must have gone home. Then the TV went on. And the phone rang. The phone rang five or six times, but it was never for me. I used up all my clean handkerchiefs. Finally, finally, the house was quiet. Everyone had gone to bed.

The clock on my nightstand was making its usual little noise, just like every other night, grinding out the minutes of my life. I was lying on my back, staring at the black ceiling, and I went a little crazy. *This day has never happened*, I thought. *I can simply* will *this day away. Aunt Marion did not tap my shoulder and call me out of the courtroom.*

For one second I almost believed I could get up and walk into Francie's room and find her there, asleep. I almost believed it. But I knew that if I believed it completely, I would be crazy. It was like I was connected to reality by a delicate white thread. If the thread broke, I would be plunged into insanity. Should I get up and go into Francie's room? If I found her there, I would surely be insane.

But I had to know. I got up from my bed, as if in a trance, and followed the thin white thread along the dimly-lit hallway to my sister's bedroom. I held my breath and switched on the light. The bed was empty.

I went back to my room, shivering and confused. I drifted into that strange interlude between wakefulness and sleep. Francie wasn't in her bed, but she *must* be somewhere. She couldn't be alive and here one minute, and then just gone forever, the next. She must be somewhere. I started to pray. I couldn't help it.

I tried to picture her in another somewhere, and then she appeared, from the shadows of my mind, slowly gaining strength and clarity. And soon another form appeared at her side. It was Jesus — the same familiar Jesus I had pictured in my prayers since my childhood. He was bending over her wheelchair, gesturing to her in a slow and patient way, a picture of gentleness and love. He had something slung over one shoulder, objects which He soon swung effortlessly to the ground, and I saw they were roller skates of shining silver. In a moment He was helping my sister to her feet, and then, magically, they were gliding along on a beautiful golden path, surrounded by pink and violet flowers and pools of clear blue water. His white robes were flowing, and her golden hair was lifted by the gentle breeze. I felt a sense of peace and joy so lovely it will haunt me forever.

It was a beautiful sight, but something was missing. As they skated by, I knew immediately what it was. I knew what it was by Francie's uplifted hand and Jesus' troubled smile. Francie wanted her crucifix, and Jesus expected me to get it for her.

13

I DIDN'T GO TO SLEEP FOR A LONG TIME AFTER that. I kept trying to bring back that lovely vision of Francie, roller-skating with the Lord, but I couldn't do it.

Could it be possible, I thought, that I had really broken through to another dimension?

I couldn't explain it. I only knew what I had to do. I had to go to Van Nuys and get the crucifix for Francie. I had to get it in time for her funeral. Somehow, I thought, the crucifix was the key.

They started getting up at five-thirty — Mom, Dad, and Aunt Marion. Dad started up the car a little after six. Mom and Aunt Marion were still scurrying around the house, flushing toilets and banging closet doors, and then suddenly they were gone, and all was quiet. I dozed off again.

When I woke up, I went, still in my pajamas, and phoned the Greyhound. There were several buses leaving for L.A. that morning, and I could take the night bus back that night. I could get the crucifix and have it for Francie before the funeral on Monday. She could show it to Jesus, and all would be well.

Everything seemed slightly unreal that morning. It was funny. I knew that I was going to go get the crucifix, that I *had* to get the crucifix. I knew that I was going to take a bus to Van Nuys and go to our old house and tell the people there exactly what I had to do — that I had to remove the bottom drawer from the closet in Francie's old room and find the Jell-O box that's been hidden there for years, waiting for this day. I knew all that, but still I didn't believe it was happening.

I went and counted my money and found that I didn't have enough for the bus ticket. I decided I'd borrow some from Gregg or Tyler. I got dressed and called Tyler.

"Hey, Tyler?"

"Yes?"

"I need to borrow some money when you come over."

"How much?"

"Well, pretty much."

"How much?"

"Twenty-five?"

There was a slight pause. "Okay."

"Do you have it?"

"Yeah. I cashed my birthday check. What time shall I come over?"

"Any time. Right now?"

"Well, hold on a sec."

She was back on the line in a minute. "I'll be there in fifteen minutes or so. I can take the car." She paused. "Are you okay, Alfie?"

She was always asking me if I was okay. "Yeah. I think so."

Gregg came over a few minutes after I had hung up the phone. He came over and knocked quietly on the back door, just like he's been doing for years. But this time, Francie was not there to say, "Oh boy! It's Gregg!"

"They leave for the airport on time?" he asked as I unlocked the screen door and let him in.

"I guess."

"Did you have breakfast yet?"

"No."

"Well, come on. Let's scramble some eggs or something."

I looked at Gregg. He's really okay, you know. Gregg really means well.

I didn't say anything about going to Van Nuys until Tyler got there. She handed me the money and kind of raised her eyebrows, but she didn't ask me what I needed it for. She's got too much class for that.

"Listen, you guys," I said a little later, as Gregg finished drying the frying pan and I put the jelly away, "I've got to go to Van Nuys today."

Gregg was hanging up the towel, straightening it on the rack, and he turned quickly to look at me. "You *what?*"

Tyler just said, "Van Nuys? What for?"

"I have to do something in Van Nuys, that's all."

They both looked at each other, but neither one said anything, because Francie had just died. I'll bet they would have acted completely different if Francie hadn't died just yesterday. But now, they acted like they were afraid of me.

"How are you going to get there?" Tyler asked finally.

"Greyhound."

"Do your parents know about this?" Gregg asked slowly.

"I'm going to leave them a note."

"Do you think you should do that?" he asked. "Just go off like that without telling them?"

I was already writing the note. *I'm taking a Greyhound bus to Van Nuys,* I started. Then I crumpled up the paper and started over. I decided I'd better not get too specific. I didn't want anyone coming after me or anything. I didn't want anything fouling up my plans.

I have to do some errands, I wrote this time. *I don't know how long it will take.*

After I finished writing it, Tyler came up beside me. "Let's see," she said.

She read the note and then she started getting nervous. She started fooling around with her hair. She always does that when she's nervous. "You can't go all that way by yourself, Alfie." She looked at Gregg. "*Can* she? I mean, on the *Grey*hound — all the way to Van Nuys! And how about getting home? How are you getting back?"

"I'm taking the night bus."

Gregg started acting nervous too. "You really shouldn't, you know, Alfie."

"Too *bad,* you guys! I'm going! You want to take me to the depot, Tyler, in the car — or not?"

"I can't." She looked at me, then at Gregg, then at me again. "No kidding. I told my mother I was only coming over here. I can't go driving all over town —"

"I'll go with you, Alfie," Gregg said suddenly. "If you have to go, then I'll go with you on the Greyhound." Then he added softly, almost to himself, "Your mother would kill me if she found out I knew about this and let you go alone."

"Hey!" Tyler said, her face lighting up. "I got it! I'll go too! Let's *all* go!"

"Now wait a minute," I started.

But Gregg and Tyler weren't listening. They were already making plans, both talking at the same time, flushed and excited.

"Wait a minute!" I said. "Hold it! You guys can't do that! You'd have to tell your parents, and then —"

Gregg was already heading for the door. He looked a little worried and his face was red and splotchy, the way some blonds get when they're upset or something. "I've got to go home and get some money and leave a note," he said. "I'll be right back."

"Listen, Gregg," I warned. "I'm *going*! If you get your mother coming over here or something, to try and stop me —"

"How can I do that? She's not even home. That's why I have to leave a note. She's out getting flowers for the church or something. But Alfie, I really wish you'd tell us the reason for this trip. It would sure make things easier. Do you have to see somebody, or what?"

"I don't *want* to tell you the reason! It's personal, that's all! And I'm not even *inviting* you guys to come along! Gees, I'm just going to go, that's all!" This was starting to get complicated.

While I was talking to Gregg, Tyler was on the phone. She saw that Gregg was about to leave and she put her hand over the mouthpiece. "Wait, Gregg!" she said. "Wait a minute!"

Gregg stood poised by the door. Tyler was finishing up her conversation. "I don't *know* why, Mom. Yeah. Okay. Yes, Mom. Yeah. Yeah. Yeah. Okay. Bye." She hung up.

"It's all set," she said. "I've got to go home and get some money. Jerry's home. He'll take us to the depot."

I started to panic. "Did you tell her?"

"Don't worry! It's okay. I told her you had some reason, and that you were determined to go, and that we didn't want you to go alone. I'm supposed to call when we get there,'' she added.

I looked at her suspiciously.

"It's o*kay!*" she said.

Gregg looked kind of surprised. "That's all?" he asked. "She'll just let you go — just like that?"

"Why not?" Tyler shrugged.

"Well, my mother is not so easy. I'll have to go home and leave her some kind of vague note like Alfie's, or she'll send the posse after me. Are we ready to leave now? You want to stop by my house with the car, Tyler, and wait while I write the note and stuff?"

Tyler nodded. "Okay."

"That's a good idea," I added. "Maybe we can make the nine-thirty bus."

I went to my room and put some stuff in my backpack. After I did that, I went around looking for my old blue jacket. Suddenly I remembered that I had left it on the back of my seat at the courthouse when Aunt Marion came in. I went and got another jacket and locked the back door. Then Tyler and Gregg went out the front door ahead of me, and I slammed it shut behind us.

That's when I saw Kurt's yellow Toyota just coming around the corner off the freeway. I reached out my arm in front of Tyler as she was starting down the front step. Then the three of us stood on the porch and watched as Kurt pulled up to the curb in front of my house. Two racing bikes were strapped to the back of the car.

He didn't shut off the motor, but leaped out of the car and reached through the open back window and pulled out my old blue jacket. He was wearing dark glasses and an orange tennis visor with the word *Wheaties* written across the front.

"Who's that?" Gregg asked.

Kurt hurried up the walk toward us.

"Hi," he said, looking at me and handing me the jacket. He just glanced at Gregg and Tyler and acknowledged them with a nod. "How are you?"

I took the jacket. "Thanks," I said. "Uh, Kurt, this is Tyler and Gregg."

"Hi."

"Hi."

"Hey!" Tyler said suddenly, "you're the kid on TV!"

Kurt looked puzzled. "Huh?"

"I saw you on TV!" Her eyes were sparkling.

"On the news," I explained.

"Oh," Kurt laughed. "That." He looked from one of us to the other with a quick turn of his head, like a bird. Like a bird with curly brown feathers. "So what's going on?"

"We're all on our way to L.A.!" Tyler blurted out.

"You're what?"

Gregg kind of shuffled his feet around and looked away, like he was anxious to get going.

And then I suddenly remembered. "Your brother's bike! You're taking the bikes back!"

"Yeah. That's right. And where are you going? To L.A.? No kidding? All of you? How come?"

"Alfie has a mysterious errand," Tyler said. "So we're on our way to catch the Greyhound."

"The *Grey*hound?" Kurt's eyes darted over us. He hesitated, but only for a moment. "Well, gee, you want to ride with me? I mean —"

"*You're* going to L.A.!" Tyler interrupted. "How *neat!*"

"I've still got to stop by my house yet," Gregg put in, concerned.

"And I have to drop my mom's car off," Tyler said. "Hey, listen, I can take Gregg by his house and wait while he writes the note and stuff, and then you guys can pick us up at my house." She looked at Kurt. "It's not far."

Kurt shrugged. "Okay by me."

"See you in a few minutes then," Tyler said, starting down the walk. "Come *on*, Gregg. Let's go!" She came back and grabbed him by the arm. "Come on!" she said. Then she shook his arm a little as they went down the walk, and said, "Hey, I'll bet when you came over here this morning you never thought you'd be ending up on your way to L.A., huh? Isn't it ex*cit*ing?" She turned and waved at us. "See you in a minute."

"Well," Kurt asked me, after we watched Tyler start up her mom's car and take off, "is that it? You taking two jackets, or what?"

"Oh," I said. I unlocked the front door again and tossed my other jacket in the hallway closet.

"What happened yesterday, anyway?" Kurt asked. "You didn't come back."

"Well, my sister died." I slammed the front door shut again.

Kurt turned sort of pale. "Jesus! Your *sister?* She *died?* Well what happened? Uh, how old was she?"

"She was eleven. She's been sick a long time." So then, on the way to the car, I told Kurt a little bit about Francie. I told him how she was born with this disease, and how she had other health problems as well, like her heart. The doctors always said she would probably die from the heart trouble before the other. It turned out they were right.

Kurt didn't say anything during my explanation. And when I finished, he just shook his head and said softly, "God, that's rough!"

We were in the car and on our way by then. It was obvious that he was pretty shaken up by what I had just told him.

"Which way to Tyler's?" he asked gently.

"Just go straight," I said. "I'll tell you where to turn. It's a mile or so."

I was on the verge of tears, so I took some quick shallow breaths. But that didn't seem to help much. I didn't want to talk about Francie any more.

So I cleared my throat and asked Kurt what happened at the trial after I left.

"Huh?" Kurt looked at me quickly. I guess he was still thinking about Francie.

"Oh. Well, it was really interesting." He wet his lips lightly with his tongue like he does sometimes. "First of all, Judge Perluss surprised everybody by saying he was ready to deliver his ruling. Most people thought he'd take a week or so to prepare it."

"What was it? What did he say?"

"He said the way the State is teaching evolution *doesn't* violate the rights of the creationists. The Science Framework doesn't have to be changed. He said all the State had to do was make sure that the local school districts were aware of the State's policy toward evolution."

"What's the State's policy?"

"Oh, you know. That they are not dogmatic — that they can't be dogmatic in the way they present evolution."

"Oh."

"Now both sides are saying they won." Kurt motioned to the back seat with his head. "There's a newspaper back there. I didn't get a chance to read it all yet." He shook his head, disgusted. "The whole thing turned out to be a big publicity stunt, just what they had planned."

Kurt was getting all wound up again. We were at Tyler's house by then, and in a minute she and Gregg drove up. She parked the car in the garage and they both went in the back door. In a few minutes they came out and climbed in the back seat. Tyler's mother waved to us from the front door.

Kurt was still talking about the trial. "I'm just sorry," he said, starting the motor, "that it couldn't have been a real *showdown* between creation and evolution on the scientific merits of each. We'd have blown them out of the water."

I didn't say anything. I was on my way to get a crucifix for my dead sister to show to Jesus.

14

"THE LAST TIME I WENT TO L.A. WAS WHEN I was ten years old and we went to Disneyland," Tyler said, when we were on our way. "What a place. I loved it."

Gregg was having trouble finding room for his legs. "I've never been there," he said, shifting around in his seat.

"Do you want me to move this seat up or something, Gregg?" I asked. "Hey Kurt, can I move this seat up?"

Kurt told me how to fix the seat, so I moved it up and also slanted the back of it so I wasn't sitting up so straight. I guess I must have been awfully tired from being awake half the night before, because after about five minutes I just couldn't keep my eyes open. Tyler and those guys were all talking about Disneyland and the Mouseketeers and stuff and I was falling asleep. It's fun to fall asleep in a car. I like how you fall asleep in little fits and starts. Everything seems to disappear for half a second and then you hear the car sounds again, but you know you've been asleep. The next thing you know, you wake up an hour later with a stiff neck.

I don't know what woke me up. We must have hit a bump in the road or something. Anyway, I sat up and stretched and said, like a little kid, "Are we there yet?"

They all laughed, and then Gregg said, "Uh, Kurt, do you think maybe you could stop pretty soon? I'd better phone my mother."

"Oh, sure."

"You really should phone yours too, Alfie," Gregg said. "She's going to be wondering about you."

Kurt turned his head quickly toward Gregg in the back seat for an instant, and then he looked at me. "What? Why would she be wondering about you?"

Tyler leaned forward. "Well, Alfie just left a note. She's being real mysterious about this trip."

Kurt put his hand to his sunglasses and turned to me with a quick frown. "You mean your mother doesn't know where you are? She doesn't *know* you're going down south?"

I nodded.

"For Chris*sake*, Alfie! What a stupid thing to do!"

He looked away from the highway, toward the frontage road. "We've got to get you to a phone! God, that's really *stu*pid, you know it?"

I felt my face turning red.

"There's a place," Tyler said suddenly pointing to the right. "Brawley's Coffee Shop. Take this off-ramp — right here!"

Kurt turned his head quickly, changed lanes, and took the off-ramp.

Nobody said anything while he pulled into the parking lot. It was one of those uncomfortable silences. Kurt was still really mad at me. I could tell. He pulled the key out of the ignition and gave me a kind of disgusted look. "You got a dime?"

159

I reached into my pocket and pulled out some change. "Yeah. I have a dime."

We all got out of the car and walked over to the phone booth in the parking lot.

"What about you, Tyler?" Kurt asked, somewhat sarcastically. "Am I kidnapping you, too?"

That made Tyler mad. "No, Kurt. My mother knows where I am. You saw her waving goodbye, didn't you?"

He just grunted. Boy, when Kurt was mad, he really let you know it. Actually, I think he kind of overdid it.

I was glad my dad answered the phone. I called collect and he accepted the charges. Kurt was leaning up against the side of the phone booth, and Gregg and Tyler were off a little way, talking.

"Where are you calling from?" Dad asked, first thing.

"Don't worry, Dad. It's okay. I have to tell you something."

"What? What's wrong?"

"Nothing's wrong. I'm on my way to Van Nuys, that's all. I have to go to our old house in Van Nuys and get something."

It was like he didn't understand me. "Where *are* you?" he asked again. "Why are you calling long-distance?"

"At first we were going to take a Greyhound," I said. "See, Gregg and Tyler are with me. It's okay, really. See, we were just leaving to go to the bus depot, and this kid I met at the trial was dropping my jacket off. He lives in L.A., see, and he was bringing the bikes back —"

"Alfie, what in God's name are you talking about? First of all, *where* are you calling from?"

I leaned out of the booth. "Kurt! Where are we?"

Kurt moved closer to me. "We're near Manteca."

"We're near Manteca, Dad. It's okay, really."

"Now, exactly *why* are you going to Van Nuys?"

"I have to get something." Kurt was standing right beside me now.

"Listen here, young lady," Dad's voice came back sternly over the phone. "No more double talk! I want you to tell me exactly what's going on here!"

Well, I knew that tone of voice. I knew I had to tell him everything. So I told him how I had dropped the crucifix in Francie's lap so many years ago and made her think it was from Jesus. When I said that, Kurt took off his Wheaties visor and rubbed his forehead with the back of his hand and stared down at his feet.

Then I said, "She asked me about it again yesterday morning, Dad." I was crying a little now. "I promised her yesterday that I'd get it for her." But I didn't say anything about the roller skates.

At first I thought we'd been disconnected.

"Dad?" I said. "Hello?"

"I'm still here, Alfie," he said finally. It sounded like he was a million miles away. "So how are you getting there now? Someone is driving you?"

"Yeah. This kid I met at the trial. Kurt. He lives in L.A., see, and he's driving back. He goes to school in Davis."

Kurt perked up at the sound of his name.

"He's there with you now?"

"Yeah, he's here. And Gregg and Tyler too. They're both here."

Dad didn't say anything for a minute. I could hear a big sigh, though. Then he asked, "When and how are you getting home?"

"The night bus, I guess. I don't know." I really hadn't

thought about getting back. I put my hand over the mouthpiece and called Gregg and Tyler over. "How are we getting home?"

"The all night bus, I thought," Tyler said.

"Yeah," Gregg agreed.

"Hey," Kurt said suddenly, "I'm driving back to Davis tomorrow. You might as well all come back with me."

"Kurt says we can come back with him tomorrow."

"But where'll we stay tonight?" Gregg asked.

"Oh yeah, that's right."

"You can all stay over at my place," Kurt said. "That would be no problem."

"Kurt says we can stay over with him," I said into the phone.

"Want me to talk to him?" Kurt asked me softly, mouthing the words.

I handed the receiver to him.

"Hello, sir? Mr. Newton? This is Kurt Rosen. Listen, I'm really sorry about this. Yes. I didn't know. Yes." He was nodding his head and listening. Then, "Well, I'm sure my parents would be glad to have them." He gave my dad an address in Beverly Hills and a phone number. "So we'll be heading back tomorrow sometime. Okay. Here's Alfie."

Kurt gave the receiver back to me and shook his head in a kind of relieved way.

I finished talking to Dad and then Gregg called his mother. It took him about fifteen minutes to explain to her what was happening.

"Let's go in and have a cup of coffee," Kurt said after that. He started walking toward the coffee shop and we all trooped along after him.

Tyler and I went to the restroom, and then we came out

and found the guys sitting at a booth. It was one of those semicircular kind of booths. When they saw us coming, they both stood up and let me and Tyler sit in the inside. Then Kurt sat down next to me. Gregg looked at us a second, and then he sat next to Tyler.

"Might as well have lunch, huh?" Gregg asked. Gregg's always hungry.

I was still feeling bad because I had made Kurt angry, and I was lonely for Francie, I guess. Anyway, we were all pretty subdued during lunch. About halfway through, Kurt took a swallow of coffee and then set his cup down in the saucer. "So," he said slowly, wiping his lips lightly with his fingers, "you decided to play God, huh, Alfie?"

Tyler and Gregg looked at me.

"What's that supposed to mean?" Tyler asked.

Kurt looked at me. "Go on. Tell them."

I didn't say anything.

"I'm talking about the reason for this trip," Kurt said. Then he added gently, "Go ahead, Alfie. Tell them. You'll have to tell them when we get there, anyway."

So I told them the whole story. Actually, it was kind of a relief, finally talking about it after all those years. I didn't tell them about the roller skates, though.

Gregg and Tyler seemed dumbfounded. "Do you think the crucifix is still there, under that drawer?" Tyler asked when I had finished.

Gregg was just looking at me in amazement. "Francie never said a word about it to me," he whispered, as if it were still a secret.

"Well," I said, "you know, it's funny, because when I forgot to bring it on the day we moved, Francie wasn't worried at all. I remember she just smiled and said, 'Jesus will bring it to me.' "

Tyler started fooling around with her napkin, tearing it into little shreds, but Gregg's eyes never left my face.

"But I knew better, of course," I continued. "I remember thinking, *Jesus can't deliver a crucifix from Van Nuys to Sacramento.*"

Gregg was tracing a circle in the little pool of water that had condensed around his Coke glass. "So it looks like you were mistaken after all, doesn't it, Alfie?" His knowing smile was just like my mom's.

I looked at him. "What? What do you mean?"

"You were mistaken! Don't you see?"

We were all looking at Gregg now. He drew himself up and took a deep breath that made him appear even larger than he was. "It's obvious that Jesus *can* deliver a crucifix from Van Nuys to Sacramento!" he said, beaming. "And *you're* the deliveryman, Alfie!"

"What a lot of crap," Kurt remarked mildly.

"Delivery*person,* you nut," Tyler said, laughing.

But I was thinking about what Gregg had said. *My God,* I thought *can it be?* Could it be possible that this whole crazy situation was planned by God, just to win me over? The simple and ironic beauty of it took my breath away.

I virtually ignored the others all the way from Manteca to Van Nuys. The whole trip was like a dream. I lay back in my seat and closed my eyes and marveled in the ways of the Lord.

But my final little sojourn in the realm of the supernatural was about to come to a dramatic close.

"Alfie!" Kurt was saying. "Alfie, wake up. We're almost to Van Nuys. Wake up."

"I am awake," I said. "Where are we?"

"We just passed Magic Mountain."

"Okay," I said, "take the Hollywood Freeway and the Victory Boulevard turn-off." I was fully awake now.

In a few minutes we were in my old neighborhood. "Hey!" I said. "The thrift store is gone! The store where I bought the crucifix used to be right there!"

"Where?"

"Right there! Where that appliance store is. Turn left at the next block, Kurt," I said. "Look! There's my old school. And there's where Patti Peterson used to live."

Kurt turned left then, and I stared with complete disbelief at what I saw. My old house was gone, and so was the house next door. In its place stood a three-story condominium with sun-deck balconies and a basement garage.

15

KURT PARKED THE CAR ANYWAY. WE ALL got out and walked in little circles, stretching our legs. I felt like I weighed five hundred pounds. It was an even worse comedown than when the kid with the pimples stepped on my foot at the healing service, and Tyler said how she bet me a million bucks Jesus didn't do acne.

"You *sure* this is where your house was?" Gregg asked stupidly.

I didn't even answer him. Tyler gave me a helpless look and shrugged her shoulders sympathetically.

Kurt was standing there with his hands in his pockets, taking deep breaths and looking at the sky.

"Well, now what?" Tyler asked after a while.

"I just don't believe it," Gregg said.

Kurt came over and took hold of my arm. "Let's go on over to my place. Are you ready?"

I shook my head. "Not yet."

"It must be a real shock," Kurt said softly. "Your old house gone —" he snapped his fingers — "just like that."

I stood there, staring at the condominium. I still couldn't believe my old house was really gone. I felt cheated and betrayed. I remember I kept looking around down the block and across the street, still searching vainly for my old house, hoping that maybe, somehow, I had merely become twisted around and confused.

Gregg was over by the curb, bending down to tie his shoelace. I watched him as he stood back up and brushed the knees of his pants in that characteristic way he has. Gregg had said that *I* was the method by which Jesus would deliver a crucifix from Van Nuys to Sacramento. I had desperately wanted to believe that, so I did. I had thought that if I could believe that, I could also believe that Francie was still . . . But wanting to believe something does not make it true. My house was gone, and the crucifix was lost forever.

I closed my eyes and silently vowed that I would never allow myself to be fooled like that again. From that moment on, I knew that I was going to rely only on my experience and my powers of reason and logic.

I looked up at Kurt. "Okay," I said. "Let's go."

As we got in the car, Tyler took one last look at the condo and said, "Well, I guess that's that. Looks like Jesus kind of got his wires crossed, huh, Gregg?"

I thought Gregg would get mad when she said that, but she has such a cute way of saying things, she can get away with a lot.

He looked annoyed, but he didn't get mad. He just said quietly, "Jesus knows what He's doing all right, Tyler. It's *people* that get confused."

Kurt got back on the freeway and in a little while he was pulling into the huge circular driveway in front of his house in Beverly Hills.

We all straggled up the walk toward the front door, Kurt in the lead.

He pressed the doorbell a couple of times, and when no one answered, he got out his key and opened the door.

"Yoo-hoo! Anyone home?" he called out. Then he motioned us in. "Come in. Come in," he said, waving his hand.

The house was quiet. "Here, sit down," he said, picking up the phone and dialing a number. "I'll see if I can find out — Hey, Eric," he said into the phone, "where is everybody? Oh. Hmm. Yeah. Well, I've got the bikes." He laughed. "Yeah, I know. I'll leave them here in the house. Okay. You're welcome. See you later, Eric."

He hung up the phone. "My folks flew over to Baja for the weekend."

Gregg was standing by the front window. "Is anybody else ready for dinner, by any chance?"

We all groaned, just to tease Gregg. But then we decided it was probably dinner time. Kurt drove us to a nice restaurant he knew about just off Hollywood Boulevard. It had about a million old clocks all over the walls, and at seven o'clock they all started chiming. Kurt said he'd take care of the check and we could pay him back later. Kurt always seems to have everything under control.

After dinner we went to the movies. That was Tyler's idea. We were just walking down Hollywood Boulevard, going back to the car, when Tyler saw this theater on the other side of the street that was showing a Monty Python movie. "Hey," she said, "let's go see that!" She loves Monty Python almost as much as she loves Doonesbury.

"Sure, let's go," Kurt said.

"Shall we just cross over right here?"

"Sure."

Before I knew what was happening, Kurt had me by the

hand and we were running across the street, running right across Hollywood Boulevard.

Kurt sat next to me in the movies. We had gotten some Cokes before we sat down, and so Kurt had his Coke in one hand and the other one was just lying there in his lap. I couldn't stand it. I wanted to hold his hand again so badly I couldn't believe it. He must have read my mind, because a few minutes after the movie started he bent over and put his empty cup on the floor under his seat and, as he sat back up, he reached over for my hand. He looked at me for a second in the semidarkness and raised his eyebrows just a little, questioning. Then he settled way back in his seat and our clasped hands rested on his thigh for the rest of the movie. I won't go into details, but Kurt's hand was made for holding.

After the show, when we were back on the sidewalk, Kurt suddenly seemed to get an idea. "Let's go this way," he said.

It was a nice Hollywood evening, clear and not too cold, with a little breeze. We strolled along Hollywood Boulevard four abreast.

"Here we are," Kurt said after a couple of blocks. "This is C. C. Brown's. A Hollywood landmark. And, get this Alfie, the *inventors* of the hot fudge sundae!"

"You're *kid*ding!"

"Nope. They invented it. It says so right on their menu."

We went in and sat down. "Everybody want one?" Kurt asked.

Gregg and Tyler said, "Sure!"

And I said, "Well, *natch!*"

The guy brought the sundaes to our table, along with four little pots of hot fudge to pour over them. Kurt pushed mine over to me. "Here you go," he said. "Just like I promised. Remember?"

Our eyes met. "Thank you, Kurt," I said quietly.

He just wouldn't look away. "You're welcome, Alfie."

Tyler broke the spell by clearing her throat and saying, "Gee! Who would have ever thought this morning that we'd be eating hot fudge sundaes in Hollywood tonight! *Strange* world, isn't it?"

We all nodded and agreed. "Really. It really *is* a strange world," we said.

When we got back to Kurt's house, we decided we'd all just camp out on the floor in the front room. It had a thick rug, and anyway we didn't want to muss up the beds in the guest room.

Kurt didn't argue. "That's fine," he said, and went in a closet and dragged out four sleeping bags, one for himself.

"Anybody want to go for a swim?" he asked. "There are all kinds of bathing suits on the shelf here."

"Hey, that sounds like fun!" Tyler said. She turned to Gregg. "A pool and everything!"

Gregg said he'd like to go, too. But I didn't feel like it. So Kurt and I stayed in the front room and talked. Kurt loves to talk, and it seems like he knows something about everything. After a while we went and made some popcorn, and Gregg and Tyler got out of the pool.

Later, Tyler started looking through Kurt's records. "What's this Monty Python one?" she asked. "*Monty Python's Contractual Obligation.*" She laughed. "What a title. I don't think I've ever heard that one. Play it for us, okay, Kurt?"

Kurt put the record on the player. It was typical silly Monty Python stuff. We were all lying on our sleeping bags then, just kind of lazing around, listening to the record and eating popcorn. It must have been almost midnight, or after.

All of a sudden, on the record, an English boys' choir was singing that hymn Francie liked so much, "All Things

Bright and Beautiful,'' but the words were different. Their clear English voices flooded the room.

> *All things dull and ugly,*
> *All creatures short and squat,*
> *All things rude and nasty,*
> *The Lord God made the lot.*

> *Each little snake that poisons,*
> *Each little wasp that stings,*
> *He made their brutish venom,*
> *He made their horrid wings.*

> *All things sick and cancerous,*
> *All evil great and small,*
> *All things foul and dangerous,*
> *The Lord God made them all.*

The song went on for several more verses. Even before they had finished singing, I realized the devastating power of that satire. Everything had finally come into focus for me — something like the feeling that had come over me when I had first understood an algebraic equation.

I was sitting up by then, leaning toward the speakers, straining to hear every word. When the song ended, Kurt reached over and turned off the stereo. I just sat there, shaking my head slowly from side to side. I wanted to jump up and shout, "Of course! That's it! That's it!" But instead I just sat there quietly, enjoying that blissful feeling of pleasure that comes when a difficult problem is solved at last.

Gregg sat up on his sleeping bag and rubbed his eyes. They were all red from the pool. He leaned his elbows on his bended knees. "That song really borders on the sacrilegious," he said quietly. "*God* isn't responsible for the way the world is today." He looked to me for support. "Isn't that right, Alfie?"

I didn't answer.

"Who *is* responsible?" Kurt asked from his corner.

"Satan, of course," Gregg answered. "Satan, and man's sinful nature. Before the fall, the earth was a paradise."

"Gee, Gregg," Tyler said seriously, "you sound like a minister or something."

Gregg looked up, surprised and pleased. "Thank you," he said with such obvious sincerity that even Kurt raised up on one elbow and turned to look at him.

I stood up and walked to the window. It was a clear night in Beverly Hills, and the stars were out in force. I thought for a minute that I should try to come up with an answer to what Gregg had said. I thought I should tell him how that song had suddenly made me realize that dividing the world into the good and the bad — and giving God the credit for the good and laying the blame on Satan for the bad — was such a sorry cop-out. I thought I should try to verbalize the sense of joy and freedom that came with the fearless and complete acceptance of the world as it really is — the bright and beautiful, the dull and ugly, and everything in between. I had been struggling for so long to understand the mystery of life and death, and of joy and suffering. I realized then that perhaps I couldn't understand it because there was no explanation for it at all.

And then I looked at Kurt. He was lying on his back, one elbow bent, his head resting on his arm. He was watching me with mild amusement, waiting to hear how I would say it. I knew then that Kurt understood, and I didn't have to say a thing.

16

WE ALL DECIDED TO GO TO DISNEYLAND on our way home. It wasn't exactly on our way home, but we went anyway.

Nothing much happened there, except that I fell in love with Kurt. I guess, really, I was already in love with him, but I just realized it all of a sudden when we were riding in one of those little people-mover things into Tomorrowland.

Of course, it changed everything. I mean, we started acting like strangers, for gods' sake.

The ride home was weird, too. Gregg started reminiscing about how we put Francie up on the coop that day with the block and tackle, and then he made some remark about how he knew she was happy now, in heaven.

I heard Kurt say something like, "Oh, shee!" under his breath.

I didn't want to come right out and contradict Gregg, but still I felt like I should say something. So I said, "Well, Gregg, I don't know about heaven, exactly, but — who knows — maybe we will see . . . maybe we'll see people who have died again, somehow. Like maybe in a black hole or something —"

"What?" Kurt interrupted, in a high-pitched, incredulous voice. *"What did you say?"*

"Listen, Kurt," I answered, "evolution may be true, but that doesn't mean scientists know everything. You even said that yourself, remember? So maybe when we die, our molecules are sucked through a black hole and reconstituted or something. I don't know — something like that. It's possible, isn't it?" I went on rapidly. "By some yet undiscovered force?" I looked at him. "I said undiscovered, Kurt, *not* supernatural."

"That's just ridiculous, Alfie," he said, dismissing me as if I were a six-year-old. He was really starting to act so superior.

I brushed a tear from my eye. "Ridiculous, huh?" I said in a small little voice, wanting somehow to save face, but not knowing how.

Kurt suddenly softened. He turned to me for a second and nudged me with his elbow. "Hey," he said in a tired voice, "maybe something like that is possible. What do I know?"

But I knew he was only trying to make me feel better because of Francie. He didn't believe it for a minute.

"I don't get it, Alfie," Gregg said. "Here you are, coming up with some far-out theory about being sucked through a black hole or something, when all you really need is to have faith in God's word . . ."

"Believing *anything* on faith is illogical and stupid," Kurt broke in. The muscles around his jaw were twitching. "And not only that, it could also be downright dangerous!"

No one said anything for a few seconds. You could just hear everyone breathing. I turned to look at Gregg. He was staring out the window and cracking his knuckles. Then he looked over at me and shrugged.

"Yep," Kurt sighed, not giving an inch. "It all comes down to blind faith, sweet reason." I guess he always has to have the last word.

It was starting to get dark by then, and we weren't even to Bakersfield yet. It would be after midnight by the time we got home. Soon we stopped to eat, and afterwards I called home.

Dad said he'd phone Gregg's mother and the Harmons and tell them we'd be home late.

"Oh, by the way," Dad said, "I finally got a hold of Mr. Burr. I called him at home. So everything's okay. He said he'd see you tomorrow at the funeral."

"He's going to the funeral?"

"Well, he said he was. I guess he thinks — well, I guess he thinks you'd appreciate it, if he came."

"Well, that's nice of him, but I've decided that I'm not going."

Dad didn't answer for a minute. Then he said, "Well, that's your privilege, of course. Uh, here's your mother."

"Alfie?"

"Hi, Mom."

"The funeral's scheduled for nine in the morning, dear. You'll probably be getting in late tonight, so I wanted to —"

"I'm not going anyway, Mom," I interrupted.

"What, darling? Not going? Why *wouldn't* you go?"

"I can't, Mom."

"Can't?" She was starting to get irritated with me, I think. "Why *can't* you?"

I took a deep breath. "I can't go there and pretend to pray.

It doesn't matter one whit to Francie whether I go or not, and I'm not going to go and be a hypocrite.''

Her voice came back, ragged and uneven. "I don't understand any of that. Why would you pretend to pray? I just don't understand you at all anymore.''

It's funny she should say that, because I was having a hard time trying to understand *her*.

Gregg and Tyler both fell asleep a few minutes after we got back in the car. Kurt turned the radio to some soft music, and I shut my eyes and started thinking about my mother, and some crazy stuff about our brains. I was trying to figure out how people could be so different.

I started to wonder, What was the norm for the human brain, anyway? Are we rational creatures, or not? Do we depend on our senses and our powers of reason, or don't we?

I thought for a long time, and finally I came to the conclusion that rationality was indeed the norm for the human brain. I decided that if I couldn't believe that, nothing I could say or do would make any sense in this world. I would be living in a madhouse.

I started thinking of the brain as sort of a small computer, all divided up into little squares or chips. It's got all these little chips that abhor a vacuum and need to be filled. Some brains are programmed to fill their empty chips with reason. But other brains fill their chips with faith. And still others are filled with a curious combination of the two. Someday I hope to figure out how that could happen. Maybe it has something to do with enzymes and brain chemicals, but I know there must be an explanation.

Suddenly I felt the car slowing down. Kurt was stopping for gas. We all sort of sat up and rubbed our eyes like sleepy children. Kurt filled the tank and then poked his head in the window. "I'm going to get some coffee. Anybody want anything?"

We all said no.

He came out in a minute with a huge cup of coffee, which I held for him until he got back on the freeway. Our fingers touched as he took the cup from me. "Thanks," he said, keeping his eyes on the road. But a second later he glanced at me quickly, and for a minute I thought he was going to say something, but he didn't.

Pretty soon I dozed off again, and the next thing I knew, we were home. Kurt stopped in front of Tyler's house and waited until she was inside before he started up again. Then Gregg told Kurt how to get to his house.

"See you later, Alfie," Gregg said sleepily. "I'll see you tomorrow."

And then Kurt and I were alone. He drove down the deserted streets, slowing at the intersections and peering into the darkness, until we came to my house.

He shut off the motor and we sat there in the stillness, listening to those little noises that cars make after they stop.

When it was completely quiet, he said softly, "Well?"

"Well what?" I whispered.

"We're here."

I nodded. "Yeah."

Then he said, "Alfie, I want to talk to you a minute."

I didn't like the sound of that. "Let's go out in the back," I said. "I want to show you something." I had a funny feeling something was wrong. I had a feeling I wasn't going to like what he had to say.

We made our way quietly in the darkness through the side gate and past the big hedge to the chicken coop under the eucalyptus trees. Then we climbed up onto the roof. He sat down close to me and put one arm around my shoulder. Then he moved even closer to me. There was a moon out, and occasionally a car or truck would pass on the freeway. The wind was gently moving the leaves. Somewhere, very far away, a dog was barking.

"Wow," he whispered. "It's beautiful out here."

I held my breath and waited.

"Alfie," he said, "I've been thinking about how I could say this to you all the way from Anaheim."

I started to get a dull, aching pain in my chest.

"It's not that I — well, the whole thing is, my God, Alfie, I'm twenty-three years old and you're just a *kid!*"

His face was close to mine and the leaf-speckled moonlight was shining on his hair. I knew he would kiss me if I made the slightest move, so I raised my hand and touched that little brown curl by his ear. I had been wanting to do that since the day I met him. Slowly, just as I expected, his other arm went around me and we kissed — a sweet, tentative, perfect kiss. My first, from someone I really cared about.

"Can't you just pretend I'm twenty-two or something?" I whispered.

He swallowed and attempted a smile. "I'd rather pretend I'm seventeen."

"But it doesn't matter."

"Oh, Alfie," he sighed, "it does matter. It's not fair to you, can't you see? You're not even out of high school, yet." He hesitated. "You haven't even had a chance to go out with old Victor What's—his—face."

I hesitated, but only for a second. "I don't care about that."

"That's what you say now. But besides, haven't you noticed how we talk? Really, Alfie, haven't you noticed?"

"Like what?"

178

"Like I'm always *telling* you stuff. You know how I do."

"Well, that's just because you —"

"It's because I'm too old for you," he interrupted.

I was determined not to cry. I was blinking back tears like mad. For one wild moment, after we kissed, I had thought, *maybe*. . . . But now I knew he meant it.

"So come on," he was saying. "It's late. You should get inside."

I wouldn't get up.

"Come on," he said tenderly. "Please, Alfie? Come on. Please don't make this any harder than it is."

I still wouldn't get up. I don't know what's wrong with me sometimes. He finally had to practically carry me off the roof. And then I wouldn't walk right. So he put his arm around me and we walked back to the house like a couple of drunks.

"Got a key?" he asked when we had made it to the door.

I nodded, but I didn't get it out. It was in the back pocket of my jeans.

"Come on, Alfie."

"Are you ever going to call me?"

"I don't know what good it would do." His voice broke then, and my heart soared. But not for long.

"Give me the key, damn it."

I reached in my back pocket and got out the key. My hand was shaking.

Kurt took it from me and opened the door. He gave me a little push, and I finally had to accept the fact that he was really saying goodbye.

All of a sudden I got very angry. "Don't push me, you big jerk!" I said, shaking loose from his touch.

He looked at me as if I had struck him. "Please, Alfie," he said, almost begging, "please don't act like that."

"Well," I answered, wanting to hurt him and just lashing

179

out blindly, "I hope you don't think you were the *first* guy I ever kissed out there."

"No, Alfie," he said tersely, without missing a beat, "and I doubt that I'll be the last."

I realized then that I was no match for him. Kurt was years ahead of me.

He put his hand on my shoulder and started rubbing my collar bone with his thumb, and I began to cry. "Come on," he whispered, "let's part friends, okay?"

The tears were streaming down my face now and I couldn't talk. I just looked at him and nodded, and he bent down and gently kissed me good-bye. Then I went into the house and closed the door behind me. Goodbye kisses are not that great. They hurt too much.

I didn't plan to have an epilogue, but it looks like that's the way it's working out. I slept late this morning, since it was Saturday, and so did my mom. Around four this afternoon, Aunt Marion and her friend from nursing school days dropped over. They had been apartment hunting all day and were in the neighborhood. Actually, I think Aunt Marion just wanted to come over and see how Mom was doing and try to cheer her up a little. It seemed to work, too, because they were all laughing about something the manager said at one of the apartments they had looked at. Then they invited Mom to go with them to see two or three more that were on their list.

Two things happened after they left.

First of all, my dad called from the motel.

"You want to go jogging?"

"When?"

"Right now."

"Well, sure."

"I'll be there in ten minutes."

I quickly put on my jogging stuff and was waiting by the window when the phone rang again.

"Alfie?"

"Yes."

"This is Victor. How are you?"

"Fine. How are you?"

"I'm . . ." he said, with perfect timing, "I'm . . . about the same." And I knew that was going to be our own private joke forever.

"Listen, uh —" he said. "They're having a special bill at the State tomorrow night — *Flying Down to Rio* and *Top Hat* — so I thought . . . well, I asked myself, now, who do I know . . . uh . . . who would . . ."

Poor Victor. There he was, trying to work up the courage to ask me to the movies, and there I was, thinking about Kurt, sitting beside me on the roof and saying, *You haven't even had a chance to go out with old Victor What's–his–face.*

I swallowed the lump in my throat with some difficulty. And then I remembered something else that Kurt had told me, about his high-school days, and I thought maybe I could help old Victor out. "Are you asking me to go with you to the movies tomorrow evening?"

"Uh, yes. Can you go?"

"I think I can," I said, as evenly as I could. "I'd like to anyway."

Just then I heard my dad's old Mercedes pulling in the driveway. "But listen, Victor, my dad's here. We're going jogging. Can I call you later? I'll ask my mom and call you back."

"Sure. Okay. That's great."

The sun was just starting to go down as I ran out to the

181

car. We drove over to the park, where there's a lighted jogging path.

"I thought maybe we could make some definite arrangements to do this regularly," Dad said, after we had run a mile or so. "Like, maybe a couple of times a week. We could set up some days."

"That would be great."

It was getting dark now, and the wind was starting to come up. I hadn't run for quite a while and I felt really out of shape. We rounded the corner by the big elm tree and the wind blew against us harder and harder as we approached old Cardiac Hill. Dad slowed down and glanced at me to see how I was doing. And then a really strange and wonderful thing happened. I looked up off the path for a moment and saw the evening star shining in the western sky, and I suddenly recalled something I had read in *Cosmos:*

We have begun to contemplate our origins:
starstuff pondering the stars.

Starstuff! My whole body seemed to respond to the call. I'm not a sinner! I'm as good a human being as I can possibly be. I'm starstuff! We all are. Mom, Dad, me — and Francie, too.

I looked over at Dad and he nodded at me, and together we raced up over the hill and around the bend.